The journalist must live with one question:

"What's the news?"

This book is dedicated to the photojournalists whose answer to that question is contained in its pages.

Andris Straumanis

The best of
Photojournalism/8

An annual based on the 40th Pictures of the Year competition sponsored by the National Press Photographers Association and the University of Missouri School of Journalism.

ABOVE: Newspaper Photographer of the Year Bill Frakes of The Miami Herald worked around the clock to record scenes of violence during a 60-hour riot in Miami's Overtown area (see p. 64).

PRECEDING PAGE: Photograph of a lone gemsbok roaming over the giant dunes of the Namib Desert was made by Magazine Photographer of the Year Jim Brandenburg of The National Geographic. It won first place in the Magazine science/natural history category.

CAL OLSON, editor
Assistant: Joanne Olson

Copyright ©1983
National Press Photographers
Association, Box 1146
Durham, N.C. 27702

Library of Congress Catalog
Number 77-81586

ISBN 0-89471-221-7

ISSN 0161-4762

Printed and bound in the
United States of America by
the Publications Division of
Jostens/American Yearbook,
Topeka, Kansas 66609

Distributed by Running Press Book Publishers, Philadelphia, Pennsylvania. Canadian representatives: John Wiley &

The best of PJ/8

Contents

Sons, Canada Ltd., 22 Worcester Road, Rexdale, Ontario M9W 1L1. International Representatives: Kaiman & Polon, Inc. 2175 Lemoine Avenue, Fort Lee, New Jersey 07024.

This book may be ordered directly from Running Press Book Publishers, 125 South Twenty-Second Street, Philadelphia, Pennsylvania 19103. Please include $1.00 for postage and handling.

For information concerning the Pictures of the Year competition, contact Charles Cooper, NPPA Executive Director, Box 1146, Durham, N.C. 27702.

FRONT COVER: Photograph of a youngster swinging away at a speed bag from a chair is part of a picture story on wee boxers by Dave Peterson of The Des Moines Register (see pps. 232-235). REAR COVER: Bob Fila of The Chicago Tribune waited for the revealing moment to make photograph of a cleaning lady who took a final look at the body of John Cardinal Cody as she vacuumed the altar before the funeral (p. 91). (Cover design by Running Press).

The Argentine ship "General Belgrano" goes down after being hit by British air attack at sea near the Falkland Islands. Fighting claimed 250 Britons, 712 Argentines and several ships on both sides before an Argentine "surrender" that forced President Leopoldo Galtieri to resign.

Anno Domini 1982:
Nothing was easy

SHLOMO ARAD, NEWSWEEK MAGAZINE

Red Cross worker carries the body of a victim of the massacre in Beirut. Some 800 men, women and children were slaughtered by militiamen. While Israel was condemned for letting Christian militiamen into the camp, Israeli spokesmen disclaimed responsibility.

The world didn't get any smaller in 1982, but it undeniably became a lot more complex. That complexity was reflected in the stories covered — and not covered — by photojournalists.

If time is a stream, the events borne on its current were the focal points for the photojournalists' concern in 1982: Wars and rumors of war; acts of God and acts of man; the tangibles and intangibles of political change and economic pressure; all the hurry-scurry of the great, the near-great and the not-so-great. What a surfeit of newsmaking events!

Most dramatic and pervasive news of the year involved arms and men: War in the Mideast, in Central America and in the South Atlantic.

Photographic coverage of the Mideast fighting was particularly intensive. Photographers were on hand to report the all-out conflict between Israel and the Palestine Liberation Organization as it ravaged its way across Lebanon. The Israelis punched through to Beirut, forcing the PLO out of the city and the country — but not out of existence.

Almost incidental, it seemed, was the massacre of some 800 Palestinian refugees in two Beirut camps by Christian militiamen. But photographic coverage of the killings laid a deep shadow over Israel's victory. Resulting world opinion raised almost unprecedented tensions between Israel and her allies, including the United States.

The growing level of the fighting in Central America captured the reluctant attention of U.S. citizens. Scores of staff photographers and freelancers contributed to the mosaic of coverage of leftist rebellions in El Salvador and Guatemala, and of bloody border clashes between Honduras and Nicaragua.

(continued next page)

A changing pattern:

(from preceding page)

In contrast, news photographers had trouble covering what Newsweek termed "an improbable war" between Great Britain and Argentina. Britain's problem was one of logistics: How to fight a war 8,000 miles from home. Logistics, plus censorship, also caused problems for photojournalists attempting to cover the war.

Photojournalists were at work on other dramatic stages, too: In Poland, where the dream of independence was taking a long time to die; in the Far East, where American photographers were becoming more acceptable (and whose reportage accordingly grew in perception); in the developing nations, whose view of even-handed photojournalism could often leave something to be desired.

But as always, the great bulk of American photojournalistic activity was centered at home. Local news was still the king. But local news was changing.

In 1982, local news involved such things as the continuing problems facing a conservative administration, and the grinding problems of an economic recession that touched every part of the country.

It was a year when Tylenol became a vehicle for mindless terrorism; when the Equal Rights Amendment died after a 10-year fight for ratification; when a growing national sentiment for a freeze on nuclear weapons became a daily and running story; when such names as John Hinckley, John DeLorean and "E.T." became household words — and images.

And all across the nation, photojournalists honed their professionalism on the whetstone of passing events: The plane crashes, the casual killings (and not so casual), the slow, relentless parade of people and weather and sports and you name it . . . all the joys and ills that flesh can support or mind conceive.

Thousands of Americans experienced the fate of these men, laid off as they came off shift at the Bunker Hill smelting and mining operation in Kellogg, Idaho. In similar waves, people stopped working all across the United States, driving the unemployment rate to 10.8 percent. Said Photographer Natalie Fobes about these Kellogg miners: "They traveled throughout the west looking for jobs, often spending their last savings. There were no jobs to be had."

FIRST PLACE MAGAZINE NEWS/DOCUMENTARY, WERNER VOIGHT, SIPA PRESS FOR LIFE MAGAZINE

Dazed survivors stumble away from the wreckage of a jetliner that careened off the end of a runway in Malaga, Spain, and crashed into a truck. Fatalities: 56 persons.

ANONYMOUS PHOTOGRAPHER FOR LIFE MAGAZINE

Three days before his death in November 1982, Leonid I. Brezhnev, Communist Party leader for 18 years, made his final public appearance atop Lenin's tomb in Moscow's Red Square. He was 75.

Early casualty (below) in the Reagan administration was Secretary of State Alexander M. Haig Jr., who stepped down as a result of internal problems. Successor: George Shultz.

WALLY MC NAMEE, NEWSWEEK MAGAZINE

A special kind of violence captured national attention in November 1982, when boxer Duk Koo Kim was knocked unconscious in the 14th round of his Lightweight WBA title fight with Ray "Boom Boom" Mancini

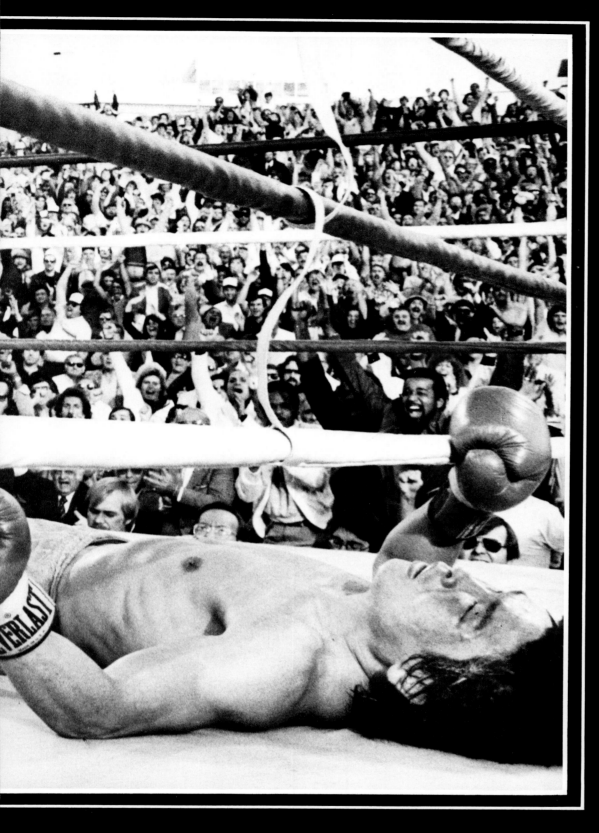

in an outdoor stadium in Las Vegas.
Duk died in a hospital the day after the
fight. His death started a debate over
the safety of boxing as a sport, and its
suitability as a spectator event. Despite
the talk, no changes resulted.

No end, no peace

Horror, combined with compassion, was the American reaction to the continuing fighting and death in the Middle East. The Israeli offensive against the Palestine Liberation Organization was a matter of the Americans' daily news diet. And American joy rose at the prospect of some resolution of the conflict when the PLO was forced out of Lebanon.

But then, American incredulity mounted when the reportage of refugee massacres began to spew out of Beirut. The unhappy realization: No end to the tensions, no peace in sight.

SHLOMO ARAD, NEWSWEEK MAGAZINE

FADI MITRI, NEWSWEEK MAGAZINE

Bodies of Palestine refugees lie on the street, above, after massacre in Chatila camps in Beirut. Recalled one U.S. photographer: "The ability of human beings to inflict incredible suffering on others . . . it will always be with me." At left, a relative mourns for the victims of the massacre.

PLO fighters (right) prepare to be moved out of West Beirut after their defeat at the hands of Israeli forces. Said Photographer David Turnley: "The football stadium where the PLO congregated to be evacuated is located near the Shatila and Sabra refugee camps where Palestinians were massacred."

DAVID C. TURNLEY, DETROIT (MICH.) FREE PRESS

Combat classics

An Israeli soldier offers water to a blindfolded Syrian captured during the fighting in Lebanon in June 1982. Photographer Reuven Castro, an Associated Press stringer based in Tel Aviv, won the George Polk Award in news photography for this picture.

RINA CASTELNUOVO, ASSOCIATED PRESS (BOTH PHOTOGRAPHS)

Two Israeli soldiers respond to fire (above) as they move towards West Beirut early in August 1982. Below, soldier at left falls after being hit by PLO sniper.

SALEH RIFAII, ASSOCIATED PRESS

18

Bombs dropped by Israeli jets (left) explode in a neighborhood on Beirut's southern fringe in June 1982. It was a two-hour air attack that Israeli spokesmen said was in retaliation for an assassination attempt on Israel's ambassador to Britain.

BILL FOLEY, ASSOCIATED PRESS

An Israeli soldier rests atop an armored personnel carrier near Beirut early in July 1982. Photographer Bill Foley continued his coverage of the war after he made this picture; three months later he made photographs of the massacre in Beirut that brought him the 1983 Pulitzer Prize for spot news photography.

Civilians paid a continuing price in the Lebanon fighting. At left, civilians load a van with their possessions in Sidon, which was damaged when Israeli forces captured southern Lebanon early in June 1982.

THIRD PLACE SELF-EDITED MAGAZINE PICTURE STORY, ROBIN MOYER, TIME MAGAZINE

SECOND PLACE MAGAZINE NEWS/DOCUMENTARY, YAN MORVAN, SIPA/BLACK STAR FOR NEWSWEEK

The PLO has been removed and the fighting has ceased; now (above) begins the long, slow process of removing the rubble and rebuilding Beirut. (Original in color)

HONORABLE MENTION MAGAZINE NEWS/DOCUMENTARY, STEPHEN R. BROWN, U.S. NEWS AND WORLD REPORT

Emotional moment (right) for PLO members as they prepare to leave Beirut. (Original in color.)

This casualty of the fighting (right) stayed on after it was over: A child burned by a phosphorous bomb is treated in a West Beirut hospital. (Original in color.)

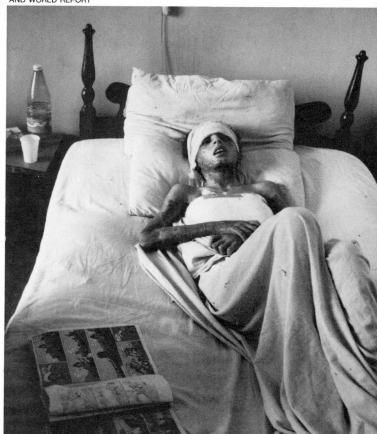

Opposite page: A Palestinian woman brandishes a rifle after the departure of her husband, a PLO fighter, who was sent to Tunisia after cease-fire in Lebanon.

PAOLO CROCIANI, ASSOCIATED PRESS (OPPOSITE)

EDWARD J. HILLE, DALLAS MORNING NEWS, ALL PHOTOS PAGES 22, 23.

Salvadoran soldier sweats it out during fighting in San Vincente.

Central American upheaval —

No end, no resolution

The agony of revolution continued to spread across Central America in 1982. Photographers faced death as they reported on the clash of conflicting ideologies through the tortured nations: El Salvador, Guatemala, Honduras, Nicaragua, Costa Rica.

In a massive report on the Central American situation, the San Francisco Examiner called it "A world of guns and machetes, where government-sponsored murder is horrifyingly commonplace.

"A world of too many bodies and too little land, where millions scratch out a dismal living and a small elite rages against mounting pressures for social change.

"A world of priests who take up arms in the name of Karl Marx ... A world of refugees and displaced persons, an estimated 1.4 million men, women and children fleeing violence, repression and grinding poverty."

The Central American upheaval had no end in 1982, no resolution. It will continue. It most certainly will spread. And news photographers will continue to report the tragedy and the horror of the strife.

Firefight in San Salvador (above): Two women scurry for cover as a Salvadoran soldier peers from the shadows.

A pair of Salvadoran soldiers share space in a C-47 with the body of a fallen comrade — and a dozen boxes of ammunition.

23

JAMES B. DICKMAN, DALLAS TIMES HERALD, BOTH PHOTOS

Election day in El Salvador

Salvadoran general elections in March 1982 were marked by guerrilla disturbances, as the revolutionaries tried to keep voters from the polls. This wounded soldier is being helped to safety during a skirmish near election headquarters in El Salvador.

Election day battles resulted in a number of guerrilla groups being wiped out. Here two soldiers move the body of a dead guerrilla. Photographer James Dickman's coverage of the fighting in El Salvador won the 1983 Pulitzer Prize for feature photography.

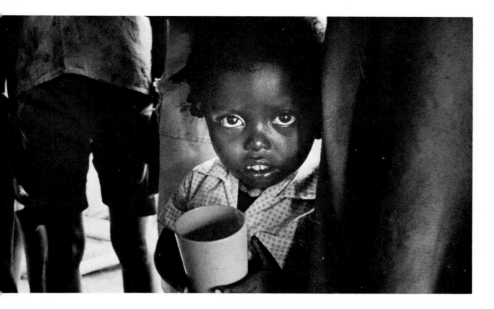

Refuge from war

Photographer John R. Storey found two groups of refugees in Honduras: Salvadorans fleeing the war in their country, and Miskito Indians fleeing forced relocation by the Sandinista government in Nicaragua. Pictures at left show Salvadoran refugees.

SCOTT R. SINES, SAN ANTONIO EXPRESS-NEWS

This is Colonia Benito Juarez, a refugee camp in Mexico that is home to some 200 Guatemalan families. There are about 30,000 refugees in 26 such camps along the Mexican-Guatemalan border: Indians fleeing from the army of Gen. Efrain Rios Montt. Photographer Scott R. Sines said "There were almost no men, just women and children. All the men had either been killed or were fighting the war."

The Nikon World Understanding Award —
'My reality was no longer valid'

Eli Reed is a staff photographer for the San Francisco Examiner. In 1982, he was one of seven staffers assigned to cover the tragic events in Central America. The team produced a 15-part, comprehensive report on what they found. As a result of his work, Reed won the Nikon World Understanding Award for 1982.

"I was sent," Reed said, "because of my previously expressed interest and understanding of Central America and the Examiner's desire to create a primer on that area for their readers."

Reed spent three months making photographs in five Central American countries. "I was exposed to a new understanding of the word 'humankind'," he said. "I saw a world that defied rational understanding, sometimes becoming clear only when you faced nose to nose what was in front of you. Personal aspirations, pain, hopelessness and death meshed inside my viewfinder."

Reed described his assignment: "I first arrived in El Salvador wide open for a 'purity of vision', prepared to capture the essence of what was happening there. I quickly discovered that my idea of reality was no longer valid. Reality became valid only when I became part of what I was photographing.

"It is real when you are crouching directly behind a soldier advancing on a rebel position, or witnessing the horror of a family confronting the grisly remains of what was once a family member."

In a story he wrote for his newspaper, Reed said: "My approach was to be totally receptive and sensitive to what was happening. As it developed, each country had a particular flavor, each was a totally different reality. But the overriding quality was warmth-friendship for strangers.

"At times, people really extended themselves, and that was interesting for me as a black American.

"Blacks are very rarely seen in El Salvador. When they do appear, they're suspected of being Cuban. And if they're Cuban, to most Salvadorans it follows that they must be communist, and if they're communist . . . what are they doing walking the streets of San Salvador?

"I always made sure my press credentials were prominently displayed."

In the fall of 1982, Reed was granted a leave of absence to become a Neiman Fellow at Harvard University.

ELI REED, SAN FRANCISCO EXAMINER, ALL PHOTOS PAGES 29-39

In Guatemala, reported Reed's newspaper, "nothing is extreme and nothing is shocking." Above, civilian militia members, armed with rifles and machetes, patrol near one city. In El Salvador (right above), the Pineres family lives in squalor Americans can't even imagine: malnourished children, the husband earning $4 to $6 a day when he works, the wife illiterate, pregnant and crippled. Right below, Nicaraguan man lives in quake-damaged building in Managua, making a living salvaging scrap metal.

World Understanding —

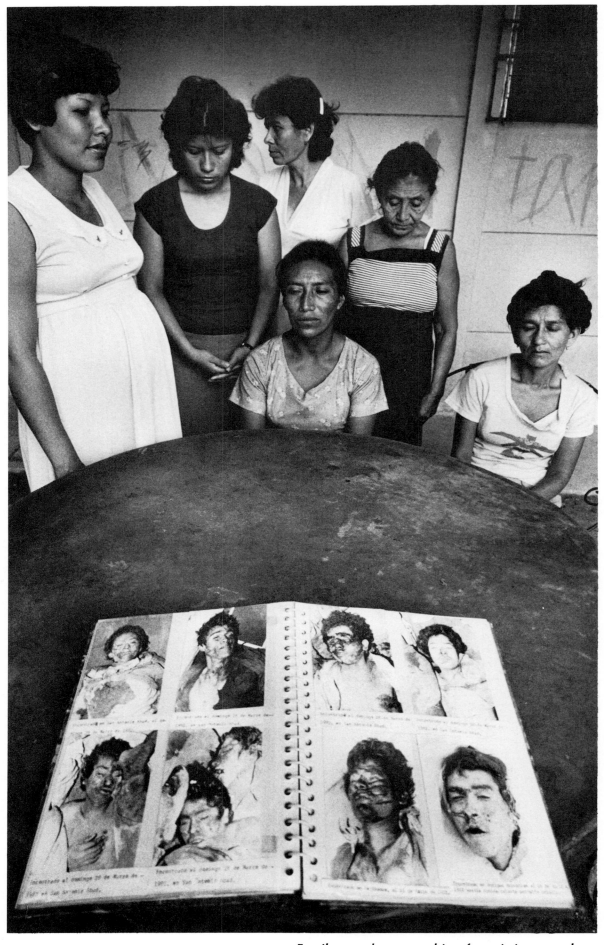

World Understanding —

Family members searching for missing people stand over an album filled with photographs of the dead in San Salvador.

32

Bodies of eight persons killed in a massacre in Sal Salvador lie in a hospital morgue. Non-combatant slayings rose as high as 300 a month early in 1982.

World Understanding —

U.S.-trained Salvadoran troops have indifferent success dealing with guerrilla troops. Here a soldier moves ahead of his company in search of guerrillas in eastern El Salvador.

Women
in the land
of macho

Poverty forces many Central
American women into prostitution.
This pair works in a casa de citas
(house of appointments) in
Guatemala City.

Female workers in a sugar cane
cooperative in El Salvador, where a
huge landless class evolved, but
where agrarian reforms aim at
putting 55 percent of the land into
cooperatives.

A poor family in El Salvador washes
clothes and bodies the way most
poor people in Central America
do: At the nearest river or stream.

World
Understanding —

The room of a teenage hooker in a
seedy section of San Salvador.

Revolution has not touched
Bluefield, Nicaragua, where this
woman and her grandson sit in the
house where she was born in 1932.

Salvadoran girl walks across a field
that is farmed by a cooperative
under the country's land reform
program.

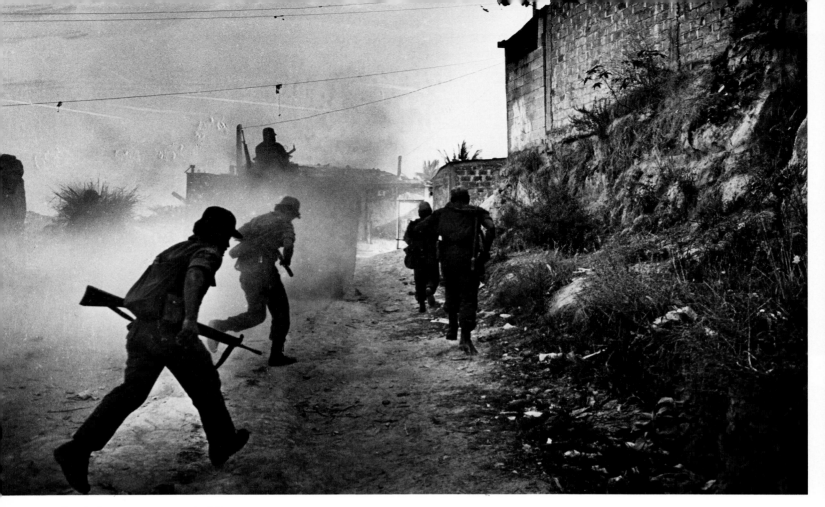

The fighting goes on: Soldiers
skirmish with rebels in San
Salvador.

World Understanding —

U.S. influence is apparent in
military dress and arms; these
soldiers guard Presidente Hotel in
San Salvador.

The Examiner's reportage called the Central American situation a "Peckinpah film brought to life." At left, a politician's bodyguard stands outside the official's specially equipped Cherokee Chief. Salvadoran politicians and ambassadors always equip their cars with frosted windows and travel with armed guards, reported the newspaper.

The ultimate photographic statement on the situation in Central America: Reed's photograph of a young woman and her infant, standing over the grave of the woman's father with the hills of El Salvador behind them.

Rain
of
death

El Chichon was a volcano time had forgotten. Its last eruption may have been more than 10,000 years ago. As mountains go, it was minor: 4,300 fet above sea level in the Mexican state of Chiapas. Closest residents are Mayan Indians, long since reduced to poverty, leading simple lives in small villages.

Late in March 1982, the forgotten volcano roared into life. Hot rocks and ash thundered into the villages. People died as they were suffocated, burned, buried in rubble. Ash filled the sky over hundreds of square miles.

After its initial eruption, El Chichon erupted several times. As a result, more than 60,000 people were evacuated from their homes.

With a reporter, Photographer Chris Johns spent four days in the stricken towns and villages closest to El Chichon. Their work was presented in a special report by The Seattle Times.

THIRD PLACE NEWSPAPER PHOTOGRAPHER OF THE YEAR, CHRIS JOHNS, THE SEATTLE TIMES

Refugees sit atop relief bags of corn, waiting for the disaster to end.

A peasant pauses (left) on the ashen road from his village as El Chichon erupts again.

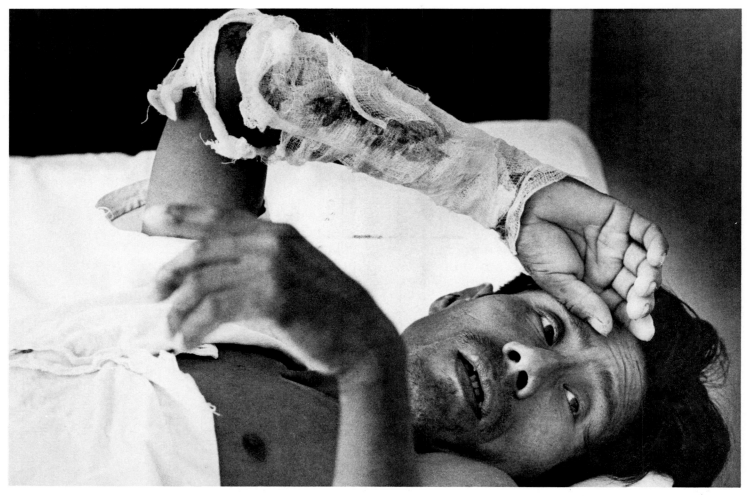

El Chichon . . .

Ramiro Aguilar-Castro (above) survived burns suffered in El Chichon's first eruption. But his wife and one son died.

Residents of the beleaguered little town of Pichucalco tried to clean up volcanic ash (below) but they couldn't stay ahead of the volcano.

*As El Chichon billows ash, a
Mexican soldier stands guard in
the abandoned village of Nicapa.*

Farewell to a princess

In March, Princess Grace of Monaco posed for an informal portrait in the living room of her Paris home. Six months later, she was dead, victim of an auto accident. Photographer Sarah Leen flew to Monaco to cover the funeral. She staked out a spot at the Palace at 6 a.m., jockeying for position among 100 photographers. Her reward was this perceptive photograph of the mourning family-Princess Caroline, Prince Rainier and Prince Albert. "When the funeral began," said Leen, "the noisy, rowdy group of photographers became the most well-behaved group I have ever worked with. As the family passed, there was only the sound of shutters and motors whirring in the wind."

SARAH LEEN, THE PHILADELPHIA INQUIRER

HARRY BENSON, FREELANCE FOR PEOPLE MAGAZINE,
RUNNER-UP, MAGAZINE PHOTOGRAPHER OF THE YEAR

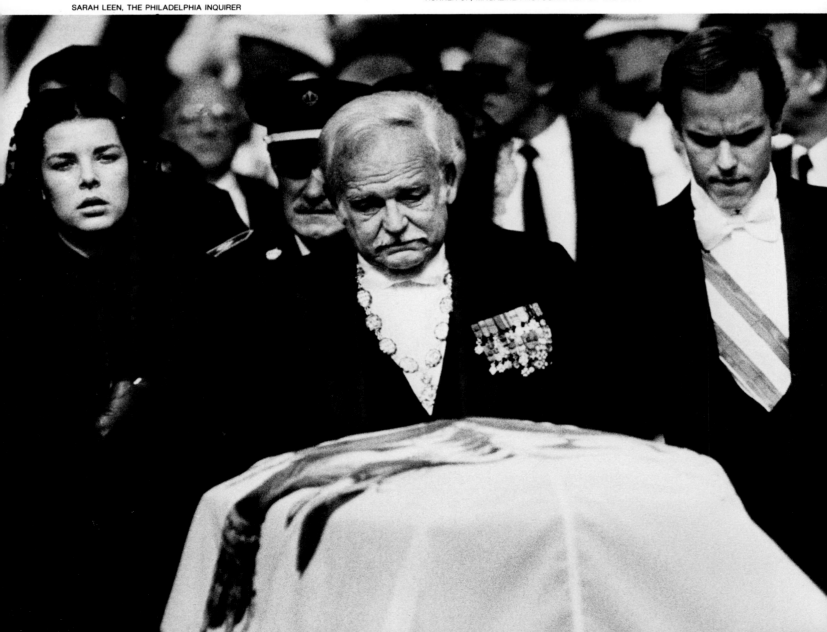

PETER R. HVIZDAK, JACKSON NEWSPAPERS, NEW HAVEN, CONN.

Goodbye, John

Comedian John Belushi was 33 when he died in a Hollywood hotel bungalow, the apparent victim of a drug overdose. Friends, relatives and fellow actors buried Belushi's body near his vacation home on Martha's Vineyard. Dan Aykroyd, who starred with Belushi on "Saturday Night Live" and in "Blues Brothers," led the funeral procession on his motorcycle. "He was the first to arrive at the graveside," said Photographer Joanne Rathe. "He just folded his arms and stared into the empty dirt."

JOANNE RATHE, THE BOSTON HERALD

Boat people: they keep coming

The flight from the Caribbean continued, especially from oppressed Haiti, where (left) manpower is so cheap it is more economical to bring mixed concrete up in buckets by the numbers instead of by machine. The refugees came by the thousands in frail vessels: More than 100 were aboard this tired craft (right). Once in the U.S., Haitians were not given political status as were Cubans. Some (below) were sent to Otisville Prison in New York state when there was trouble at the Florida detention camp. Speaking only French, unused to cold weather, they were separated from other prisoners. In view of their uncertain future, Photographer John Long thought their march in to the fog "was particularly appropriate."

NATHAN BENN, NATIONAL GEOGRAPHIC MAGAZINE (ORIGINAL IN COLOR)

LEFT, TIM CHAPMAN, THE MIAMI HERALD

JOHN LONG, THE HARTFORD, CONN., COURANT

Joblessness: the big story

Call it the year of hard times, 1982- a year when the nation's unemployment rate hit 10.8 percent. So many Americans hadn't been out of work since the Depression of the 30s. The tragedy of joblessness touched almost every American to some degree. It reached into every city, into every stratum of the nation's society. It was the most pervasive, continuing local story of the year.

JOHN F. SHECKLER, STANDARD TIMES, NEW BEDFORD, MASS.

In New Bedford, Mass., the rate of unemployment rose to 12.7 percent, and the permanently jobless used one line at the unemployment office (left), seasonal workers another. In Seattle, Wash., a job call for 21 openings packs a union hall (right). These are ship scalers, 900 strong, mostly black, working a day every week or two. Below, homeless men wait for news of work at a St. Louis, Mo., job agency that specializes in day labor.

ALAN C. BERNER, THE SEATTLE TIMES

FIRST PLACE GENERAL NEWS, KAREN ELSHOUT, THE ST. LOUIS POST-DISPATCH

Thousands of unemployed persons flocked to San Diego (right), where facilities like the City Rescue Mission served 550 meals a day to the dispossessed. Photographer David Gatley said the newly jobless "want to survive, and they held onto their dreams of recovering from the pitfalls of our troubled economy." A tough story to cover, Gatley added: "Their eyes reach into your soul and heart. You question their survival and their futures."

Unemployed —

They called it "Tent City, U.S.A." (left), and it was one of the most media-oriented manifestations of unemployment in the country. Just outside Dallas, Tex., it got wide coverage. Here's one of the families who occupied the facility.

Joblessness came home to half a dozen newspapers, which cut staff as they consolidated or ceased publication altogether in 1982. When the Philadelphia Bulletin folded, it ended a 134-year tradition in the city, and spawned a huge farewell party in the newsroom. "This bulletin board (below) was in the downstairs lobby," said Photographer Steven Zerby, "but no one seemed to want to look at it or think about having to find another job."

STEVEN P. ZERBY, VINELAND, PA., TIMES-JOURNAL

JOB PLACEMENT INFORMATION

The Wall:

On a quiet weekend in November 1982, the Viet vets finally came home.

Oh, they'd been back physically for eight years, a decade. But their real homecoming came in Washington, D.C., during dedication of the Vietnam Veterans Memorial — The Wall.

It is a memorial almost as controversial as the war it commemorates. But it is THEIR memorial- their Wall- and they came to mark the occasion.

They wore the old uniforms. They came singly and in groups. And they marched, and

they remembered. They accepted, and were accepted.

For photographers who covered this event, The Wall was almost as emotional as it was for the veterans. Recalls Photographer Jebb Harris: "It became hard to be detached as I watched men and women break down into tears as they found the name of a friend or relative on The Wall. Grown men hugged and wept.

"On some occasions, after making a picture, I had to wait to get the names; to give them time to stop crying, and so that I wouldn't start."

53

The Wall

Steve Slaughter, ex-Marine, responds to the cheering crowd.

The body English of these two ex-Green Berets tells the story.

55

JEBB HARRIS, COURIER-JOURNAL AND LOUISVILLE TIMES

The Wall

While thousands massed at The Wall, above, Photographer Jebb Harris felt that "The presence of those missing was heavy in the air." Couple in photo at right, said Photographer William Saunders, "was there for almost 10 minutes, just holding each other as if it would erase all past feelings and remembrances of the war." Veteran leaning against The Wall, far right, is Jerry Connors, who later wrote Harris that controversy over The Wall is appropriate: "It seems to run parallel with the controversy over the war itself." He concluded his letter by saying, "I love my country and all its citizens. If I were asked to fight again, I would not hesitate."

ARKANSAS

WILLIAM SAUNDERS, THE WASHINGTON TIMES

SECOND PLACE GENERAL NEWS, JEBB HARRIS

Tragedy by air

Air traffic continued to carry most of the nation's travelers in 1982 and, as in most recent years, provided some of the most tragic and dramatic news stories of the year. The heart-stopping drama of a major air tragedy was brought home to millions of Americans who watched live television coverage of rescue efforts after one airliner accident.

It happened on Jan. 13 when Air Florida's flight 90 took off in a snowstorm from Washington, D.C., and crashed into a Potomac River bridge. Seventy-eight people died in the crash, but many were saved by the efforts of heroic passers-by.

Photographer Bernie Boston made this general view of the crash scene. Boston said he was at his office transmitting routine photographs when he was alerted to the crash. "The site was more than three miles away," Boston said. "Traffic was not moving, so the only way to get to the crash was to run ... it pays to stay in shape."

BERNIE BOSTON, THE LOS ANGELES TIMES

Plane Mishaps

Five days after the loss of Air Florida 90, salvage crews (left) hoisted the tail section of the aircraft from the Potomac River.

Less tragic, but certainly eye stopping, were incidents involving private planes. Above, a private pilot from Michigan made a perfect emergency landing on an interstate highway near Williamsburg, Ky., after he lost oil pressure. And at Independence, Mo., eight inches of rain fell in a few hours Aug. 8, creating a situation at the airport (right) that Photographer John J. Spink called an "aquaport."

LARRY RUBENSTEIN, UPI NEWSPICTURES

ROBERT STELLA, FREELANCE, BRAINTREE, MASS.

Plane tragedies

Ten days after the Air Florida crash in Washington, D.C., a World Airways flight 30 went off the end of a runway at Boston's Logan Airport, plunging into the Boston Harbor. Two passengers were killed, 208 rescued. Photographer Robert Stella was among newspeople taken by shuttle bus to the scene five hours after the accident. He recalled that another photographer "turned to me and said, 'We live for this kinda stuff.' "

Photographer David Leeson was among eight news photographers his newspaper sent to cover the crash of a Pan American World Airways jet-liner in New Orleans July 9. The crash killed 154 persons and spread fire and devastation over a four-block residential area.

"I wasn't prepared for such a shocking scene," Leeson said. "Nothing seemed real ..." He shot picture of priest administering last rites (below), but wasn't sure he had it, because he'd damaged his lens. "I followed the priest around, hoping to see another last rite," he said. But he'd made his picture the first time.

DAVID LEESON, THE TIMES PICAYUNE/THE STATES-ITEM, NEW ORLEANS, LA.

Police battle blacks in Miami — again

Late in December 1982 a young police officer shot and killed a young black during a "pool room search" in a Miami video arcade. That was the beginning of a three-day series of riots and bombings: police officers against blacks.

While the death of 20-year-old Nevell Johnson triggered the violence, observers said the real cause of racial unrest was a number of frustrations that exist in Miami's Overtown area.

Some of the news photographers who covered the event worked almost continuously through 60 hours of unrest.

"Riots are no fun," said Miami Herald staffer Bill Frakes, 1982 Newspaper Photographer of the Year. "This was the third riot I've covered at The Herald . . . It is important to record what is going on, but it is also important to make sure that you're covering the news and not becoming a part of it. The cameras always manage to stir up the crowd."

WALTER MICHOT, FT. LAUDERDALE NEWS AND SUN/SENTINEL CO.

MICHAEL duCILLE, THE MIAMI HERALD

Young blacks who overturned an automobile (above) run from police tear gas. At left, the mother of Nevell Johnson reacts when doctors tell her he will not live.

Miami riots —

In full riot gear, right, Miami police prepare to meet street violence. Below, looters under arrest.

Protesting black, left, comes to grips with police officer. "The dimension of violence, death and destruction was not as great as 1980," Photographer Bruce Gilbert said. "But everyone knows now, how a small spark can inflame . . ."

HONORABLE MENTION GENERAL NEWS, JOSE M. MORE, THE CHICAGO TRIBUNE

His second year

GH SCHOO

At left, President Reagan took center stage in a suburban Chicago high school to answer questions from students. Below, the quintessential Reagan, responding to reporters as he heads across the South Lawn of the White House.

IRA SCHWARTZ, ASSOCIATED PRESS

The bloom was off and the long haul was on: It was the second year of Ronald Reagan's presidency and problems were mounting.

The big domestic worry was the economy, primarily the dilemma of a gradual recovery hand in hand with the highest postwar unemployment rate (10.8 percent).

Reagan nonetheless weathered it all: Foreign travel, problems with Congress, growing resistance to Reaganomics, the departure of Secretary of State Alexander M. Haig Jr., and an off-year election in which Democrats picked up 26 seats in the House.

And as the year wound down, the chorus grew: Will he run again in 1984? Reagan kept his own counsel on that one.

His second year —

'Shut up!'

Hottest, shortest remark of the president's second year came in October, as he gave a pep talk to a group of Republican candidates in the East Room of the White House. A California congressional hopeful, Gary Arnold of Santa Cruz, rose to accuse Reagan of deserting the political right. The president countered first with facts, then with humor. When that failed, he shook one finger and shouted, "Shut up!"

Photographer Bernie Boston said he had looked around for California people and had spotted Arnold. "While Reagan was speaking, my eye was also on Arnold as I wanted to tie the two together to enhance the possibility of getting the photograph in the paper," Boston said. "When Arnold interrupted the president, my camera was ready, and I was able to get a picture that others did not."

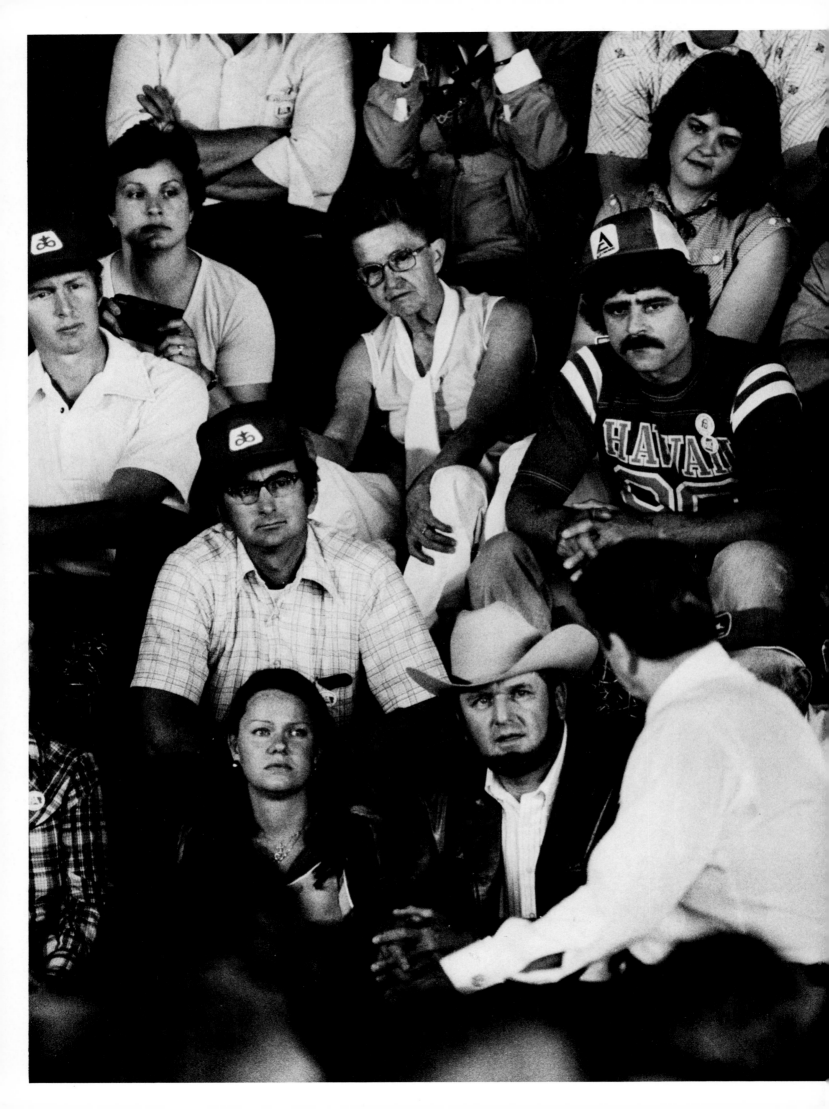

His second year —

Unsmiling Pennsylvania farmers (left) had many questions for President Reagan during a stop in dairy country, questions about the poor economy, high interest rates and protectionist legislation. A month later, in June, the president went riding (above) with Queen Elizabeth II on the grounds of Windsor Castle. The president and his wife visited three days in Great Britain. Back home in October, President Reagan was greeted by a simple message (right) on a visit to Great Falls, Mont., to campaign for a GOP legislative candidate.

Acts
of
God

Floods and fires, windstorms and quakes: These are the stuff of spot news, and the news photographers' ultimate function.

And there was news of this kind in plenty during 1982. Among the stories: The spring floods in Ft. Wayne, Ind., where hundreds of volunteers worked long hours to lay in sandbags to buttress earthen dikes that were turning mushy from the water.

Heroes of the flood were Ft. Wayne high school youngsters, including this trio.

SCOTT GOLDSMITH, THE COURIER-JOURNAL AND
LOUISVILLE TIMES

Fire and flood make for personal tragedy- and compelling photos. At left, helicopter fights an out-of-control fire at Florida's Lake Okeechobee. The chopper flew over Photographer Cecilia Conrad as she was leaving the area: "Fortunately for me."

Below, a resident of Rome, Ill., rowed his dinghy (and Photographer Pete Souza) down the town's main street during December floods throughout the state.

At right, Photographer Anthony Suau used wide angle lens and backlighting to emphasize grocery store losses when a dam on Colorado's Lawn Lake gave way in July, flooding the business district of Estes Park.

Randy Rumrill sobs as he searches for the body of his father in the rubble of the elder Rumrill's home. Structure was destroyed in mud slides that hit northern California in January 1982. Photographer Jean Dixon, then working for the Palo Alto, Calif., Peninsula Times, said, "It was one of the most tragic scenes I've ever had to cover. I just went numb and kept shooting . . . and then I wanted to go up and hug the poor guy."

TALIS BERGMANIS, THE KANSAS CITY STAR

Photographer Talis Bergmanis spotted fire-gutted building on his way to work one sub-zero morning. He shot outside, then inside. "But I needed a person for scale, and there was no one around," Bergmanis said. After a chilly 30-minute wait, a workman arrived to inspect the remains, and Bergmanis had the picture.

As far as Photographer John J. Gaps III was concerned, his picture of a fire-wracked, ice-festooned frat house at Iowa State University was largely a matter of "F/8 and be there." Still, after Gaps covered the blaze through a long afternoon and evening, he was not satisfied. So, when the windchill hit 40 below in Ames, Iowa, that night, Gaps said he "kept setting my alarm so I would get up every two hours to start my car, just to make sure it would turn over in the morning, because I saw the potential for the ice shot in early light." Obviously, Gaps' car did not fail to start.

JOHN J. GAPS III, THE OMAHA, NEBR., WORLD HERALD

--- and acts of man

When a small band of Ku Klux Klan members planned a rally in Washington, D.C., they were greeted by several thousand shouting, rock-throwing anti-Klan protesters. The demonstration quickly got out of hand. Here, a nightstick-swinging police officer knocks a suspected looter through a downtown store window.

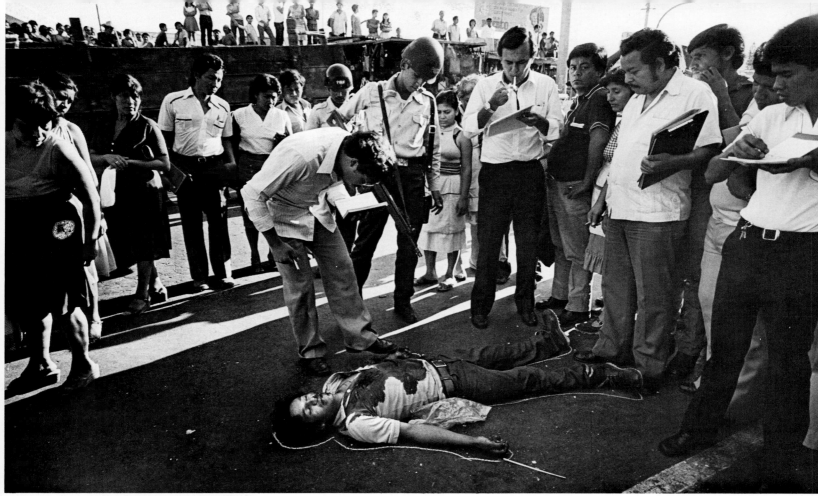

FIRST PLACE SPOT NEWS, MURRY SILL, THE MIAMI HERALD

In attempting to rob a feed store, two men ran into a guard with a machine gun. Both men died. Above, a medical examiner blocks out the position of one corpse. Audience included police, auxiliary police, newspaper reporters and the morbidly curious.

Cochise County sheriff's deputies tried to serve traffic warrants on members of the controversial Christ Miracle Healing Center and Church near Tucson late in October. In an ensuing battle, two members of the all-black church were shot to death and dozens of lawmen and church members were wounded. Fight, below, took place just before the shooting started.

THIRD PLACE NEWS PICTURE STORY, JAMES L. DAVIS, THE ARIZONA DAILY STAR, TUCSON

When an early-morning drinking party led to murder in a Minneapolis park, Photographer Darlene Pfister took the call (7 a.m.). She spent an hour at the scene before friends of the victim returned. Pfister used a 300 mm lens to record their stunned grief (above) "to avoid intruding upon them."

A handcuffed 18-year-old kisses his wife goodbye (right), while a San Jose detective waits to take him away. The couple and their two children had been homeless. When the Mercury carried a story of their plight, a probation officer recognized the man as an escapee. "The couple called a reporter and me," said Photographer Karen T. Borchers. "While we were there, the police moved in."

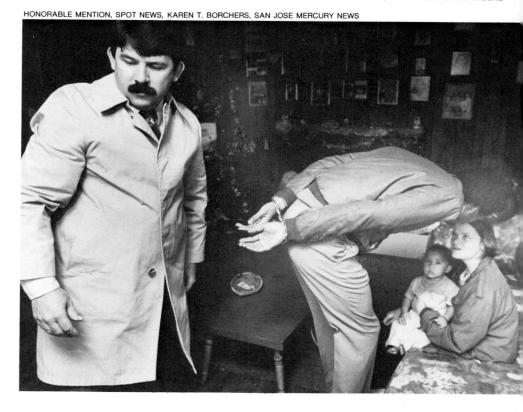

A Detroit detective (white suit, left) waits to escape from burned office building. He keeps one hand on man who went on a 90-minute killing and fire-bombing rampage that left one dead and 38 injured. That's the man's distraught brother at the right. (Original in color.)

SECOND PLACE, SPOT NEWS, MARY SCHROEDER, DETROIT FREE PRESS

After four persons died in a fire at the Conrad Hilton Hotel in Chicago in May, a waiter served cold drinks to the hot firefighters. Said Photographer Anne Cusack: "It was an unusual moment and an ironic conclusion to a tragic news event."

HON. MENTION, GENERAL NEWS, ANNE CUSACK, CHICAGO TRIBUNE

When Chicagoans began dying from poison-laced Tylenol in September, it spawned similar acts and public outcry all across the country. Above, Sophia Czyz, whose two brothers and sister-in-law died from the poison, comforts her mother during triple funeral. Photographer Robert A. Reeder returned from vacation to be assigned almost immediately to two of the so-called Tylenol funerals. Reeder's reaction: "Welcome home!"

A peace rally in June drew half a million persons to New York City's Central Park. And it was indeed peaceful. Said Photographer Anacleto Rapping: "It involved people who came in pursuit of pleasure and those who came with a commitment to a cause."

JIM MAHONEY, GLOUCESTER, MASS., DAILY TIMES

Arrow-pierced swan evaded Gloucester, Mass., rescue squad attempts to capture it. It later died. Photographer Jim Mahoney's most vivid impression: "The blind cruelty and stupidity of the act ... It escapes me how anyone could bring themselves to kill a harmless bird."

Photographer Olga Shalygin doubles as a critical care registered nurse, and takes her camera to her second job. This man was brought in after a domestic quarrel. Said Shalygin: "He was awake, alert and complaining of hunger." She got his permission to make this picture. Patient was released from the hospital a week later after surgical removal of the knife without complications.

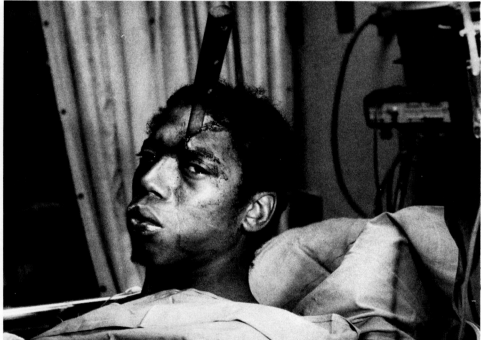

OLGA SHALYGIN, LONG BEACH, CALIF., PRESS-TELEGRAM

OVERLEAF: 4,000 people said "I do" when the Rev. Sun Moon tied the knot in a mass marriage at New York's Madison Square Garden. In this photograph he blesses the 2,000 couples as they enter for the ceremony.

VICKI VALERIO, THE PHILADELPHIA INQUIRER

BRUCE CRUMMY, THE FORUM, FARGO, N.D.

It got to the point that pictures of cars inside buildings came in clusters. Clockwise from top: Speedster hit K Mart store in Moorhead, Minn., at 40 mph; in Wichita, manager of a convenience store considers the second car in a month that plowed through front window; in Las Vegas, householder watches removal of auto from the living room; in Fort Lauderdale, a 20-year-old with no driving experience put a 1 1/2-ton truck into a living room, after leaving a trail of wrecked cars and angry drivers.

ROBERT C. BREIDENBACH, WICHITA, KAN., EAGLE-BEACON

MICHAEL O'BRYON, THE MIAMI HERALD

RON LONDEN, THE SUN, SAN BERNARDINO, CALIF.

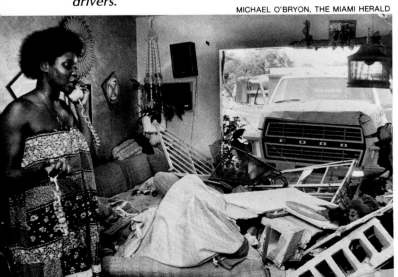

Stranded truck driver grabs for rope thrown by tow truck driver after the tractor went through a guard rail 75 feet in the air on Chicago's Stevenson Expressway.

Occupants of the cab seem remarkably cool, below, as firefighters consider their problem in an incident in Philadelphia.

Trucker Jack Browning, above, gets an arm round Firefighter Mike Sewell an hour after his rig slammed into a 45-foot hangover on I-59 in downtown Birmingham.

PAT SULLIVAN, THE SUN/DAILY HERALD, BILOXI, MISS.

Bodies of prisoners who died in a fire await identification outside the Harrison County Jail in Biloxi, Miss. Twenty-seven prisoners died, and at least 45 were injured in the early-morning fire Nov. 8. Blaze was started by a mental patient being held in a padded cell. Victims were killed by toxic fumes from the burning polyurethane padding.

Cleaning lady in Chicago's Holy Name Cathedral pauses for a final look at the body of John Cardinal Cody. She was vacuuming the altar for the funeral service April 29. Photographer Bob Fila kept his camera on the cleaning lady as she worked. "I knew she would look up," he said. "And she did . . . for a split second." Cardinal Cody's final years were marked by controversy, with a federal grand jury investigating charges that he had diverted up to $1 million in tax-exempt church funds to a life-long friend.

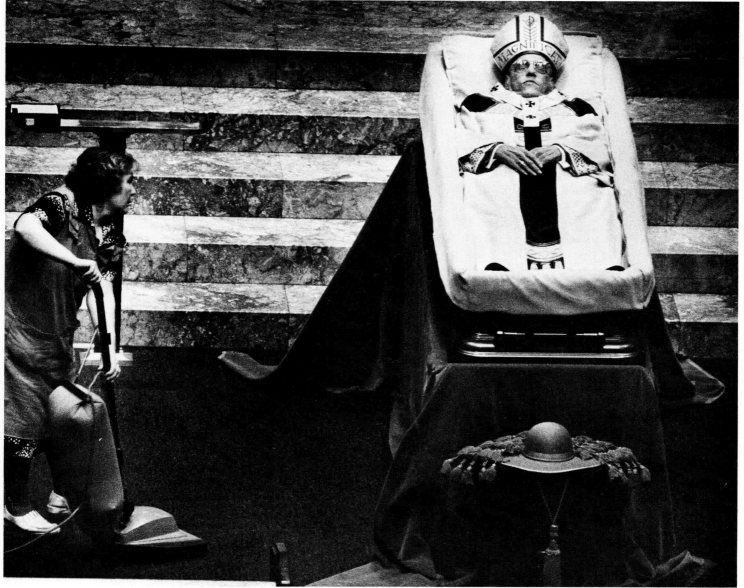

Depression Deja Vu:
The new breed of hobo

BY MICHAEL WILLIAMSON
The Sacramento Bee

In 1933, the Depression forced men to ride freight trains in search of work. Fifty years later, the paralyzed economy caused history to repeat itself.

Ever-increasing numbers of people wind up on the freights. They travel in search of work, or because they lose their homes. Most of the "new breed" hobos were just average, hard-working people with jobs. But once thrust into the world of unemployment, they get desperate. What starts off as simply a free way to travel and look for work ends up as an entire change in lifestyle. Many degenerate quickly.

The new breed live in a twisted world ruled by animal instincts- the need for food and shelter. It's also a world full of danger, crawling with desperate men armed with clubs and guns ... and railroad "bulls" who beat hobos for wanting to ride the trains.

My motive for doing the story is simple. I want to make people aware of how bad it really is out there ... whether they be the politicians who control the purse strings or just common folks who could show more sympathy and lend a helping hand.

The fact is: People are suffering.

(Photographer Williamson teamed with Reporter Dale Maharidge to report on the new breed of hobos. After their story appeared in the Bee, the pair rode the rails for another three weeks compiling a photo essay for Life. And in March 1983 the pair set out on a three-month trip around the country seeking material for a book to be published by Doubleday.)

MICHAEL WILLIAMSON, SACRAMENTO BEE (ALL PHOTOS PAGES 92-103)

Special judges' recognition, Nikon World Understanding Award

Hobos walk to the jungle at the railyards in Klamath Falls, Ore.

Rail rider (above) waves to other 'bos from his perch on "piggyback" car whizzing through California's Central Valley. At right, traveler finds boxcars aren't the only way to ride; he's at home in a car carrier on its way back to Detroit.

The new breed

Three men, above, wait for a train in an off-limits area. All three perk up at the sound of a train headed their way.

At left, David is hopping a freight for the first time in his life, and is doing everything wrong. First, he doesn't know most hobos don't hop moving trains unless they really must. Second, this train is going too fast.

David is at a critical point. If his foot misses that lower bar, it will shoot under the wheel- a "giant salami-slicer," as one old-timer called it. Even veteran train yard workers lose legs this way.

A day in the life of . . . Ken Gibson, who in 1981 lost a job in Dodge City, Kan. He spent months looking for work, but found that at 39, he's over the hill in a tight job market. This day, Ken hops a freight out of Salt Lake City, Utah, heading for Denver, Colo., still looking for work.

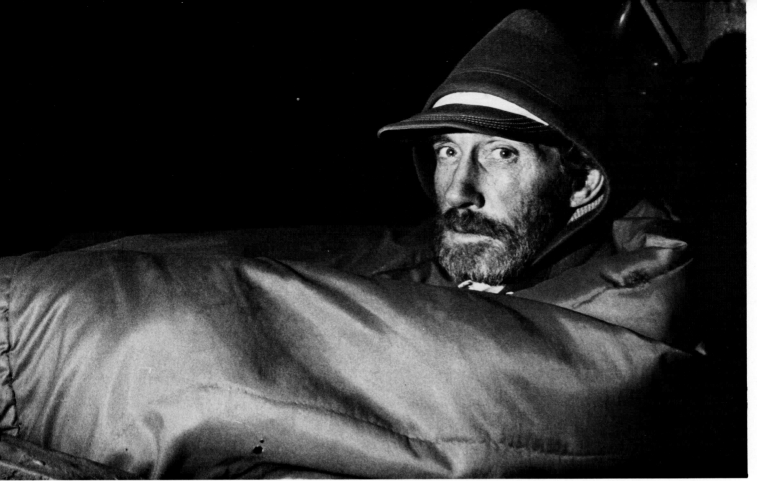

Ken huddles in sleeping bag through a cold night.

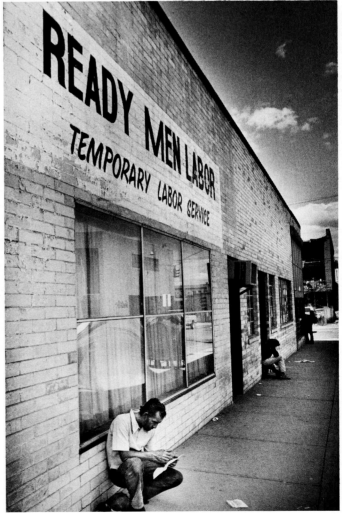

"Never thought I'd be this poor," Ken says (above), ignoring the beauty of the Colorado River Canyon. In Denver (right), he fills out job application at a labor office, trying to pick up a temporary job. But there is no work here, either.

In the Feather River Canyon (above) on the way to Oregon from California. Wayne is legally blind and Lisa is a former prostitute.

A day of firsts for Tony Hillard (right): The first time he got food stamps and the first time he ever rode a freight. As he ate the pickles he bought with the stamps, Tony explained he was heading back to Oklahoma. An oil driller who'd been laid off, Tony came to California looking for work, but couldn't find any.

The new breed

Not all hobos ride in boxcars. Grain car platforms (above) are popular, too.

Supper in a Denver jungle; for Martin it's "hobo stew" made from fat and vegetables found in a nearby dumpster and cooked in a broken tackle box found floating in the South Platte River.

Jungle in Portland, Ore., is typical of many in that city. There are people living under just about every bridge.

The new breed

David and his girlfriend share the warmth of a fire with another man in an abandoned building in Sacramento. They'd been staying in the Western Pacific railyards, but were kicked out. Police later drove them from this building.

For Sid (below) home is this spot under a railroad bridge in Klamath Falls. He's an unemployed lumberman.

Couple at left is leaving California, bound for Oregon.

Fred is a middle-aged forklift operator from Chicago. He's been on the road seven months, wound up next to the tracks in Fresno, Calif. He has given up.

The new breed

The blizzard of '82 took New Englanders by surprise; after all, it didn't arrive until April. This is a scene, would you believe, on Main Street in downtown Hartford.

O dreaded words —
'Get me a weather shot!'

That same New England blizzard that struck Hartford also hit Boston, where this pre-Easter shopper had to contend with (a) freezing lily, and (b) wind-torn umbrella.

New England did not suffer alone in April 1982. This jogger, wet but game, persevered in Denver.

. . . and it snowed . . .

Looks like the same road as in photo at left, but it's a weather shot from Illinois.

BRAD GRAVERSON, THE DAILY BREEZE, TORRANCE, CALIF.

They called it "the day the rain fell sideways" in Torrance, Calif. Photographer Brad Graverson said the winds exceeded 60 mph. He made photograph (above) from car.

Spring in Springfield, Ill., also brought 60-mile winds. Photographer Chris Covatta found wind-buffeted pedestrians (right) a block from his office.

... and it blew

CHRIS COVATTA, THE STATE JOURNAL-REGISTER, SPRINGFIELD, ILL.

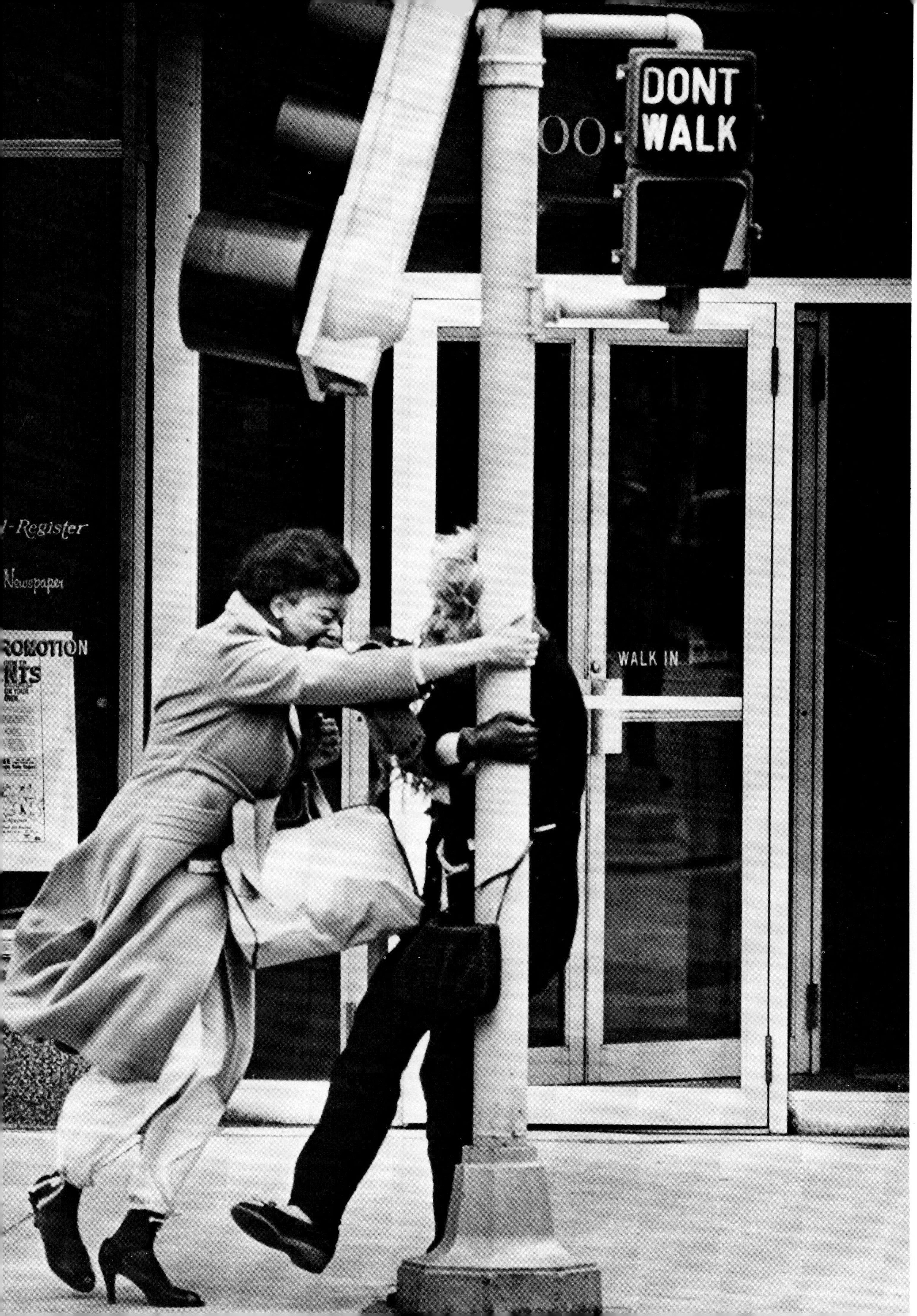
DONT
WALK
WALK IN
Newspaper

The wonderful world of features

SECOND PLACE FEATURE, MICHAEL J. BRYANT, SAN JOSE MERCURY NEWS

Oh, my goodness

Five-year-old Jessica Hammel got sick and tired of waiting for her time to perform during the dance school recital. So she got involved in the coat rack and some un-dancer-like contortions. Friend Robin Waites reacted. And then, said Photographer Michael J. Bryant, "Robin went and told their dance teacher."

Oh, my God

Dick Moorhaus is not only chief of police in Waldo, Fla., he's the town's keeper. Here's his reaction when the town's only working police car broke down as he was chasing a speeding van. No, they couldn't get it started. Yes, the van escaped. Said Photographer Bill Wax: "I rode with Moorhaus off and on for a year or so ... He lost two of three cars to mechanical problems."

STEPHEN CROWLEY, THE PALM BEACH, FLA., POST

How black-and-white can photography get? That's a Florida condominium, above, a California cucumber field, below, and a new arrival at the Metro Zoo in Miami at right.

JANICE GORDON, THE CHULA VISTA, CALIF., STAR/NEWS

WILLIAM SNYDER, THE MIAMI NEWS, RIGHT

DENNIS MC DONALD, BURLINGTON COUNTY TIMES, MOORESTOWN, N.J. (LEFT)

When Philadelphia, Pa., scheduled a parade of sails during the city's 300th anniversary celebration, Photographer Dennis McDonald couldn't get space on the official press boat: "Our paper wasn't significant enough," said McDonald. So he got on a commercial boat which, he said, gave him a different perspective than was available from the press boat (left).

Photographer James Ruebsamen said the 1982 U.S. Festival at Devore, Calif., was an event of superlatives: These are workers, right, building the biggest temporary stage in the world-more than seven stories high, 300 feet long and equipped with a 300,000-watt sound system.

JAMES RUEBSAMEN, LOS ANGELES HERALD EXAMINER (RIGHT)

High hopes and a low crowd count developed when UCLA played Cal State Long Beach at the Bruins' new regular season home- the Rose Bowl. The stadium will seat 106,000 persons- only 45,000 showed.

Loneliest place imaginable is a boat dock in the winter. Photographer Steve Koger spied a figure walking the docks, made this picture. "I think we were the only two people around," Koger said.

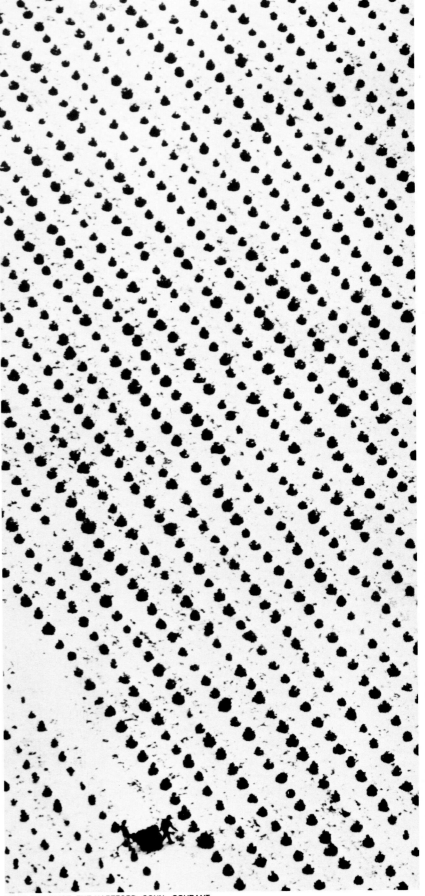

Photographer Tony Bacewicz cut a Christmas tree for his family at a tree farm. He was so taken with the symmetry of the situation that he flew over the facility a day later to photograph it.

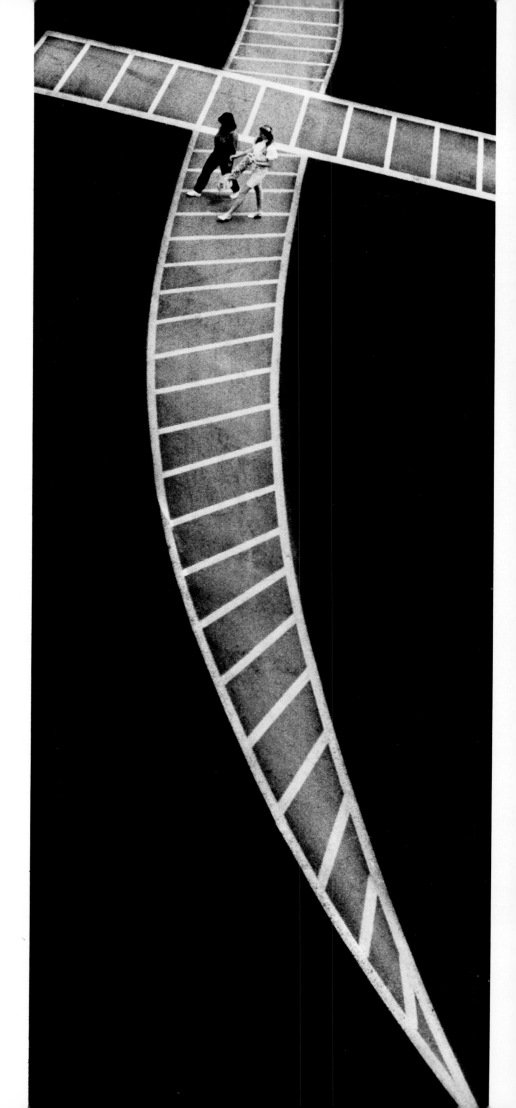

Given 15 minutes to come up with a feature picture for the local news page, Photographer Michael Rondou ran across the street to a new shopping mall, where he found fresh paint on new asphalt. Two frames, judicious dodging: assignment complete.

MICHAEL RONDOU, LONG BEACH PRESS-TELEGRAM

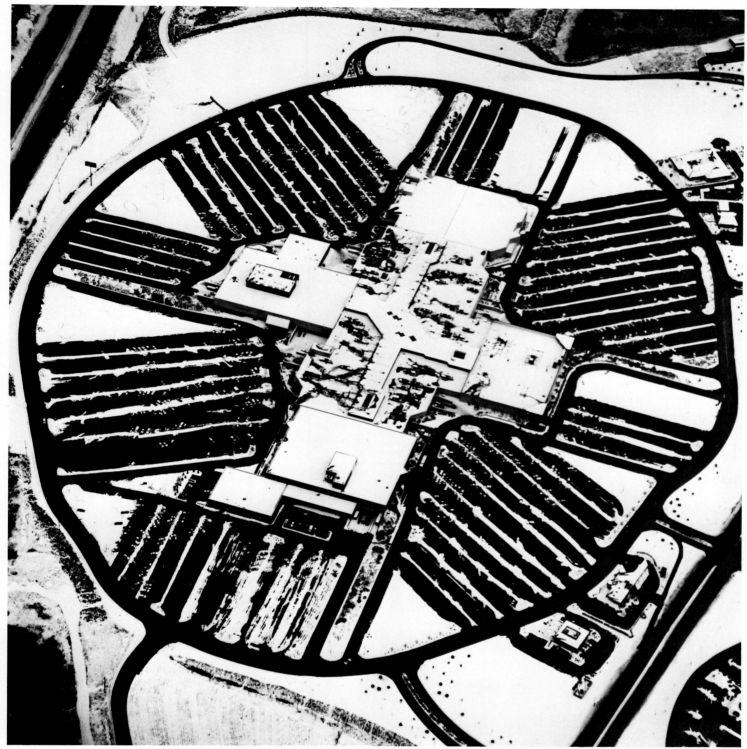

BILL KIGHT, COURIER-JOURNAL AND LOUISVILLE TIMES

Snow-covered shopping mall in Florence, Ky., caught the eye of Photographer/pilot Bill Kight as he was flying to another assignment. Kight has 600 flying/photo hours — everything from shuttle take-offs to train derailments, but, he says, "I never tire of looking at the world from the air."

OVERLEAF: Photographer Mark Randall was going to cover a baseball game, but he needed a feature photograph, too. When he saw two boys fishing in a creek in downtown Bradenton, Fla., Randall knew he had the day's feature.

MARK RANDALL, THE BRADENTON, FLA., HERALD

HONORABLE MENTION, FEATURE PICTURE STORY, JUDY GRIESEDIECK, THE HARTFORD, CONN., COURANT

The Hotel Hartford

People have driven by the Hartford Hotel for years. But these days, few venture inside. The facility once was a typical middle class hostelry. Now it houses the dispossessed: welfare recipients, alcoholics, elderly, the mentally ill. Photographer Judy Griesedieck hoped to spend several weeks on the story, but had only three days: The hotel was to be sold. Griesedieck's goal: "To show these people as human beings who might soon be out on the streets. I was disgusted that anyone would live in these conditions. But I grew to understand why. They have a sense of community and one common bond .... they have no place else to go."

Photographs and news clippings add a personal touch to 60-year-old Joe Calistro's room (above) in the Hartford Hotel. At left is Walter C. Forestry, a resident of the hotel for eight years. He's waiting in a hallway for his depilatory-type shaving cream to take effect; he can't use a razor because his hands shake too much.

Hotel Hartford —

They have little money and no means of transportation, so residents of the Hotel Hartford stay close to home. At right, Pop Bates, a six-year resident, gets together with a friend in his room. Below, the well-worn lobby is a sanctuary for all the tenants. Said Photographer Griesedieck: "The Hotel Hartford may be bleak, but the streets are bleaker."

The days run together for residents who spend all their time inside a hotel room with only a TV set for company. But the immediate problem of this man and others was solved when the hotel was sold to a man who will leave it as is ... for a while.

It makes us all go 'round

When he needed a Valentine's Day picture, Photographer Wippert recalled sign on a supermarket. Yes, it's a set-up, shot specifically for editorial illustration.

Photographer Najolia was assigned a weather shot, found this couple (below), kissing in front of the newly-painted motto on the wall at Wrigley Field. "This," said Najolia, "beats a weather shot . . ."

BILL WIPPERT, BUFFALO, N.Y., NEWS

DOM NAJOLIA, CHICAGO SUN-TIMES

PAUL S. HOWELL, THE TIMES, SHREVEPORT, LA.

JACK LENAHAN, CHICAGO SUN-TIMES

Pet monkey exchanges a lick for a hug during an animal blessing at an Episcopal Church in Shreveport, La. Love? Who knows: Hugger and lickee were complete strangers, reported Photographer Paul Howell.

A hot day in July on Chicago's 12th Street Beach, yet this couple found their own little island of isolation until Photographer Jack Lenahan unlimbered a 300mm lens.

At 17 months, Joseph Earl Luster learns about light, playing with the blinds in his parents' bedroom. Photographer (and father) Bill Luster said the picture "is very important to me personally ... Since he was born, my photography has changed radically."

It was a nice fall day, so Photographer William Daby went to the zoo on enterprise, "figuring it ought to have something to offer." The sounds of excited children drew Daby to the observation window at the polar bear pool. "I watched and shot for half an hour," he recalled. "People came and went, and all were mesmerized by that beautiful bear."

FIRST PLACE FEATURE, WILLIAM K. DABY, PROVIDENCE, R.I., JOURNAL-BULLETIN

A striking scene- which only proves that beauty is in the eye of the artist, in this case Photographer Louie Psihoyos. The photograph shows a mountain of burning garbage that rises more than 200 feet out of the sea in Manila. Psihoyos ranged the world to produce a feature on garbage, which he titled "Urban ore." His thesis: Garbage is not only a problem, it can be profitable, a way of life and, as in this case, paradoxically beautiful.

FIRST PLACE MAGAZINE SELF-EDITED PICTURE STORY,
LOUIE PSIHOYOS, NATIONAL GEOGRAPHIC MAGAZINE

NEWSPAPER PHOTOGRAPHER OF THE YEAR, BILL FRAKES, THE MIAMI HERALD (BOTH PHOTOS)

These two reaction photographs were made by Bill Frakes, newspaper photographer of the year. Photo above was made to illustrate a feature on swimsuits. Said Frakes: "Women are more overt about watching men. It's a pleasant role reversal." Picture at right, titled "40 years ago," is important, said Frakes, "because it capsulizes the story of an era in a Miami Beach neighborhood ... An aging Jewish population being supplanted by young Cuban refugees. It also addresses the tireless theme of the conflict and contrast between young and old. Finally, it looks at the way women appraise each other's physical characteristics."

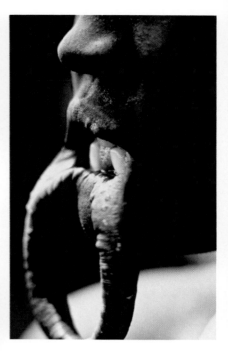

These two photographs are from a feature titled "People of the Dusty Swamp" — residents of the Southern Sudan in Africa. These are Surma women, remnants of one of the weakest native groups in Africa; barely 400 survive, after centuries of capture by slavers and attack by alien warriors. Marriageable Surma women cut their lower lips and stretch them around plates. It is a sign of pulchritude.

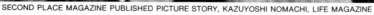

Marie Osmond was married amid much media hoopla. At right, she gets ready to have her wedding portrait made. Double truck photo of Anita Morris, below, was featured in a layout titled "Lines from the Chorus." The star of the Broadway hit, "Nine," Morris is quoted in the cutlines: "I know that I can be a star ... back home in Carolina, when there was a part to be had, all they did was call me, and I'd go, take the part and be the hit of the show ... (In New York) I've had some crushing disappointments ... Now I think I'm ready to do what I was supposed to do."

RUNNER-UP MAGAZINE PHOTOGRAPHER OF THE YEAR, HARRY BENSON FOR PEOPLE MAGAZINE

THIRD PLACE MAGAZINE PUBLISHED PICTURE STORY, BARBARA BORDNICK, FREELANCE FOR GEO MAGAZINE

THIRD PLACE NEWSPAPER PHOTOGRAPHER OF THE YEAR, CHRIS JOHNS, THE SEATTLE TIMES

Happy threesome was photographed at the Pendleton Roundup in Oregon. Photographer Chris Johns has attended since he was in high school. "This trio seemed to illustrate the wild atmosphere of the event," he said.

The Marine (left) was only an escort to the models in something they called "A Salute to American Fashion" in the San Francisco City Hall. And his hand strayed, undoubtedly innocently. "But he was quickly called on the carpet," said Photographer Lee Romero.

LEE ROMERO, SAN FRANCISCO EXAMINER (LEFT)

THIRD PLACE MAGAZINE SPORTS, TOBEY SANFORD, LIFE MAGAZINE

Essay on body builders included double truck use of this well designed, well planned photograph.

Photographer Diana Walker got all five Kennedy Center Honorees for 1982 on one sofa. From left, George Abbott, Benny Goodman, Lillian Gish, Gene Kelly, Eugene Ormondy.

THIRD PLACE MAGAZINE FEATURE, DIANA H. WALKER, TIME MAGAZINE

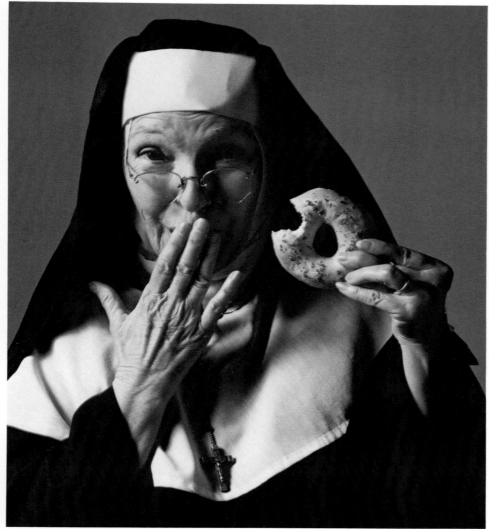

THIRD PLACE FOOD ILLUSTRATION, GEORGE WEDDING, SAN JOSE MERCURY NEWS

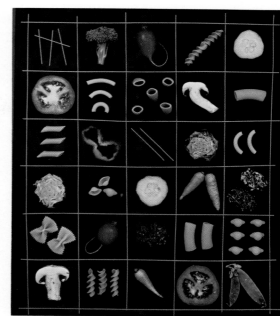

FIRST PLACE FOOD ILLUSTRATION, PAT MC DONOGH, FT. MYERS, FLA., NEWS-PRESS

To illustrate a feature on cold pasta salad, Photographer Pat McDonogh didn't shoot the usual place setting. Instead, he took the salad completely apart. It took six sessions, McDonogh said, "making me think it was snakebit."

Thrust of the feature was that bagels are for everyone these days. Photographer George Wedding's photo made the point.

Photographer Thomas Nebbia, on a journey through mainland China, made this photograph, below, along the Li River in Guilin, a region famous for its eroded limestone hills. The peaks reminded Nebbia "of dragon's teeth."

The problem: How to illustrate a feature on light wine. Photographer Craig H. Hartley did it with a feather.

THIRD PLACE FOOD ILLUSTRATION, CRAIG H. HARTLEY, THE HOUSTON POST

THIRD PLACE MAGAZINE PICTORIAL, THOMAS NEBBIA, NATIONAL GEOGRAPHIC

After a Colorado spring hailstorm, Photographer Marty Medvedik made this picture of 73-year-old John Koehler checking damage on his property. When Medvedik learned it would be Koehler's 50th and final year of farming, he returned many times during the following crop season to record Koehler's twilight experiences.

Cutlines are hardly necessary with Photographer H. Peter Curran's photograph of a priest administering confession to a Yap Indian in Micronesia.

In movements as stylized as a minuet, neophyte butlers balance wineglasses on their heads. It's the way they learn to carry their shoulders straight and keep their posture irreproachable.

FIRST PLACE MAGAZINE FEATURE, H. PETER CURRAN, THE NEW YORK TIMES MAGAZINE

SECOND PLACE MAGAZINE FEATURE, THOMAS HALEY, GEO MAGAZINE

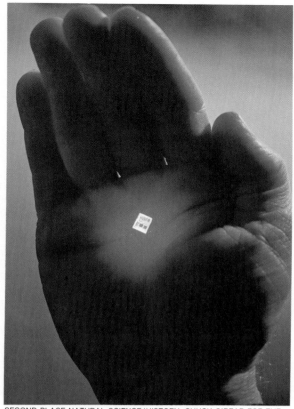

Almost lost in the palm of a hand,
a silicon chip is the heart and brain
of the new computer age.

A pilgrim visits the world's largest
sitting Buddha, 231 feet high,
carved out of a cliff at the
convergence of three rivers in
Loshan, China.

SECOND PLACE NATURAL SCIENCE/HISTORY, CHUCK O'REAR FOR THE
NATIONAL GEOGRAPHIC

HONORABLE MENTION, MAGAZINE PICTORIAL, JODI COBB, THE NATIONAL GEOGRAPHIC

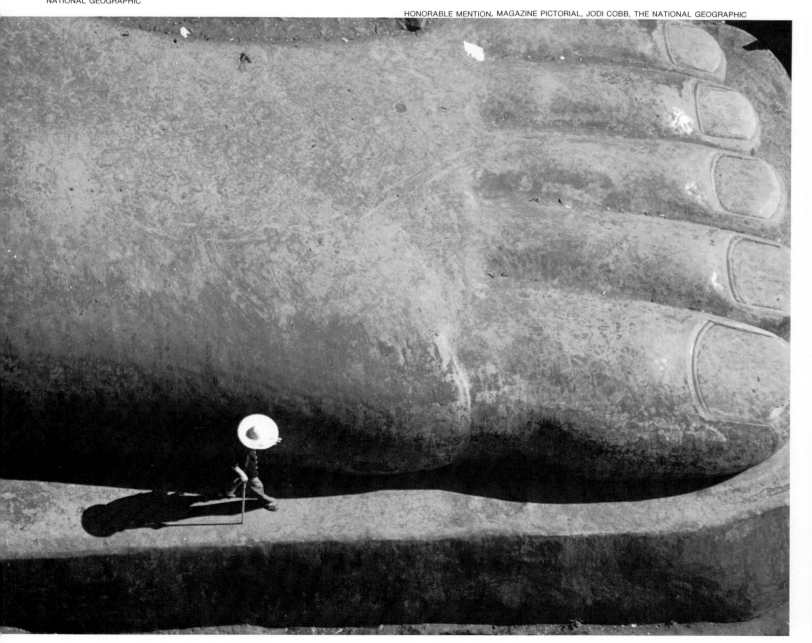

The assignment was to produce a picture page on women in the Army. But the subjects all were brought into headquarters. Solution: Pose one against a WWI-era mural.

The assignment was to illustrate a subject that has not received much attention: The issue of the unwed (and vanishing) father.

San Francisco Mayor Diane Feinstein and Fire Chief Andrew Casper submit to a test of fire sprinklers. They got what they wanted: lots of smoke, lots of water, lots of publicity. Photographer Eric Luse said his first reaction was: "A silly assignment." But, he concluded, "drawing people's attention to the life-saving value of fire sprinklers ... that is not at all silly."

HONORABLE MENTION FEATURE PICTURE, ERIC LUSE, SAN FRANCISCO CHRONICLE

THIRD PLACE PICTORIAL, PAT CROWE, WILMINGTON, DEL., NEWS-JOURNAL

It was an exceptionally foggy day, and Photographer Pat Crowe stopped at the park before going to work in the morning. He shot for 20 minutes to get this photograph.

HONORABLE MENTION PICTORIAL, DICK VAN HALSEMA JR., FLORIDA TIMES-UNION AND JACKSONVILLE JOURNAL

The show must go on, on one side of the curtain. But the cleanup must go on, too. And given that sheer curtain between performers and janitor, the audience, said Photographer Dick Van Halsema, Jr., was never the wiser.

The Ervay Shine and Domino Parlor

FIRST PLACE NEWSPAPER FEATURE PICTURE STORY, MICHAEL S. WIRTZ, THE DALLAS TIMES HERALD

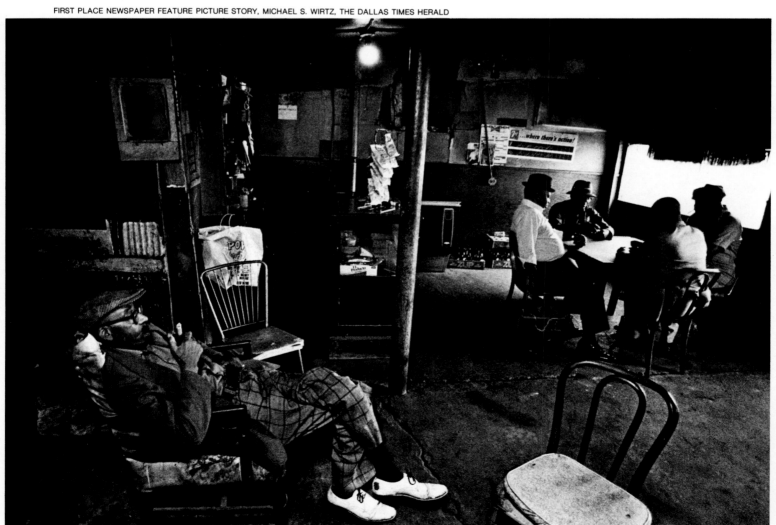

It is a small corrugated tin building that has seen better days. It looks out of place near the modern skyscrapers on the Dallas skyline.

It used to be Joe and Juanita's Cafe, then a fruit stand. Now, it is a gathering place for old men who like to play dominos.

Rooster Neal, 76, started the parlor 14 years ago. He opens it every day. But most of the time the chairs sit vacant. Saturday is about the only time Rooster shines shoes.

At night, a dozen men will show up to play or to hang out. Sometimes the clacking of dominos and the laughter and the arguments continue until dawn.

Rooster's clientele range from 75 to 80 years old. Last year, he lost 10 customers.

Willy Jackson gives a shine to one of his infrequent customers.

the Ervay —

Rooster smokes a cigar in his pipe
as he watches his customers play.

It takes a lot of cigarettes to pass the time between customers at the Ervay.

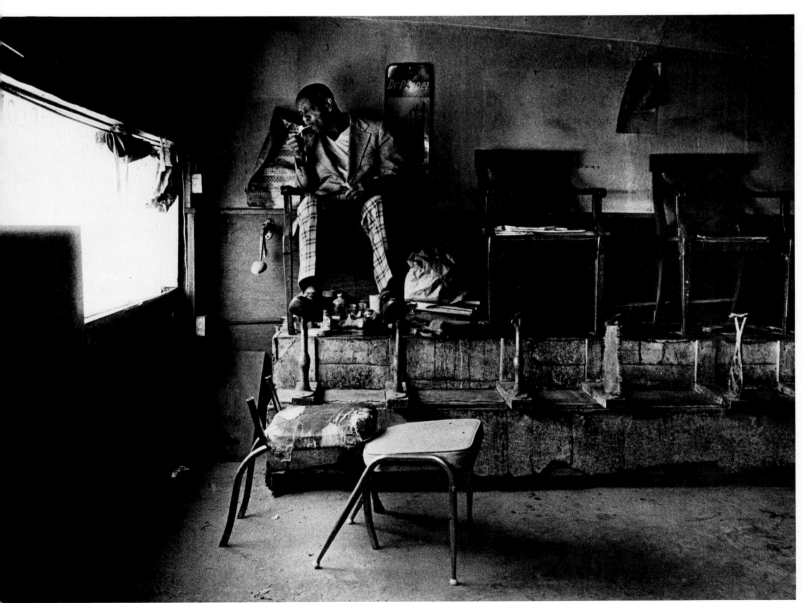

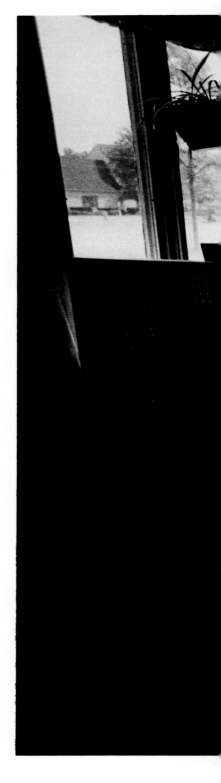

Myra: just a lady, please

By 6:30 most mornings, Myra Pledger has eaten breakfast, her lunch is packed and she's waiting for the rest of the world to catch up with her. There are two jobs to work, swimming classes to teach, a night class at a community college, monthly dances at a recreation center, and volunteer work at the Cerebral Palsy Club.

Says Myra, "I help the handicap."

Medical statistics show that Myra is one of every 1,700 people born with Down's syndrome, a genetic imbalance producing physical defects and mental retardation. But these facts have never slowed her down.

At 33, she lives at home with her parents at Virginia Beach, Va.

"I'm different," says Myra. "I'm a lady. The only thing I don't like is when people yell at me on the phone or don't treat me like a lady."

Photographer Karen Kasmauski feels "the wonderful thing about Myra's life is it reflects so clearly that retarded citizens can and do have useful lives."

FIRST PLACE FEATURE PICTURE STORY, KAREN KASMAUSKI, VIRGINIAN-PILOT/LEDGER STAR (ALL PHOTOS PAGES 150-155)

During her first months on the job as custodian in a local church, Myra carried pictures of a broom and a dustpan. "I don't need it any more," she says. "I know where everything is." At left, Myra's at breakfast with her mother, Lorraine, and her father, Carl.

Myra's a lady

Myra's on the move from dawn until long after dusk. Above, she waits for a ride to work. At right, she helps out in an afternoon swimming class. And in the evening, below, she dances with Malcolm Bohanon at a Halloween party.

One mental health specialist says Myra "has that rare capacity to make people feel better for being around her." Here she cuddles with niece Marindy Stinson, 15 months.

Myra's a lady

At the Cerebral Palsy Club, Myra helps Earl Congelton, 58, with a gardening project.

What makes Myra so special? "Maybe," says her mother, "the answer is that when she looks into the mirror she doesn't see what we see. She sees what's really there."

SECOND PLACE FEATURE PICTURE STORY, NEIL B. MC GAHEE, MINNEAPOLIS STAR AND TRIBUNE (PAGES 156-161)

The brothers

It started out, for Photographer Neil McGahee, as an interesting but not very remarkable assignment: a photo feature about two elderly bachelor brothers, Charley and Wilhelm Eilers, who still clung to 1920s farming methods near New Prague, Minn.

The Eilers were born in the same house that they lived in for 75 years. They never married. They chose to work the land by the time-honored method of horse-drawn machines.

Together they worked the rich soil, growing their crops: corn, oats and beans. Through

Charley

Wilhelm

the years they worked as a team, alternating the heavy labor, and carrying out their individual chores. Although mechanized equipment began making farm work easier, the Eilers chose to stick with the methods they knew best.

Photographer McGahee first noticed the brothers when he drove by their farm on a muddy spring day and saw them plowing with their horses. He returned for photos and interviews and arranged to do more.

But then, suddenly, Charley died, and McGahee's story took a wrenching twist.

The brothers: *Wilhelm and Charley pause from their labors for a simple lunch in the kitchen. It seemed an unchanging way of life. But Charley had a stroke.*

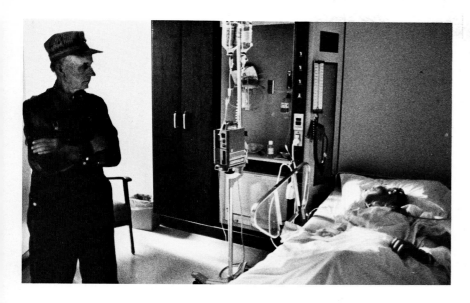

Wilhelm watched stoically as his brother lay in a coma following the stroke. Nine days later, Charley died, leaving Wilhelm alone for the first time in his life.

The brothers

Wilhelm quietly grieves the loss of his brother. He clutches a kitten that had wandered to the farm, and weeps. A few days later, Wilhelm went back to the fields to try to work the land by himself. "I'll do whatever I can to stay here," he said. "I don't want to have to go into town. I don't like town."

THIRD PLACE FEATURE, CHARLAINE BROWN, ORANGE COUNTY (CALIF.) REGISTER

When Photographer Charlaine A. Brown was assigned to photograph a male wet T-shirt contest, she knew her paper never would run photographs of the contestants at work. She did a 180 instead, made picture (above) of spectators reacting to the on-stage activity.

Photographer Michael Budrys caught it all (above right) when Karen Shanle heard she'd won $1 million in the Illinois state lottery.

Floridians who support the Equal Rights Amendment demonstrated when they heard the state legislature wouldn't ratify the ERA. Said Photographer Maggie McGinley: "Some women hugged, some cried, but they all joined for one last show of support, and this is when I took the photograph" (lower right).

MICHAEL BUDRYS, THE CHICAGO TRIBUNE

MAGGIE MC GINLEY, MIAMI, FLA., FREELANCER

163

A bird is a bird is a ... striking design, as in the photograph above, or an anthropomorphic statement, as in Photographer Joel Radtke's portrait of an emu at right.

POSTED
NO HUNTING, FISHING, OR TRESPASSING

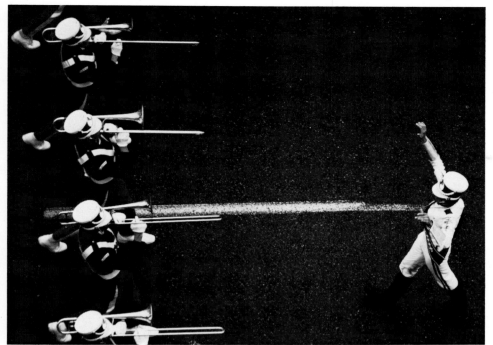

FIRST PLACE PICTORIAL, SCOTT GOLDSMITH, COURIER-JOURNAL AND LOUISVILLE TIMES (ORIGINAL IN COLOR)

STEPHEN F. RINGMAN, SAN FRANCISCO CHRONICLE

When Photographer Scott Goldsmith was assigned to shoot Louisville's Kentucky Derby Parade, he staked out on the roof of the newspaper building and waited until the drum major and the line on the pavement were right.

Photographer Stephan F. Ringman positioned himself to get runners coming and going during a marathon race from the San Francisco Bay Bridge to San Francisco's Golden Gate Bridge — all with the city's skyline as a background.

*U.Z. Gibson is a tire salvager —
but only a certain few oversized
types interest him. So he's going
through a county landfill to claim
them. Photographer Mark Edelson
had scant seconds and a 300mm
lens with which to make the
picture.*

MARK EDELSON, HOLLYWOOD, FLA., SUN-TATTLER

South beach: where dreams die

South Beach is a 1.74 square mile slice of Florida's Miami Beach: 232 blocks and 103 alleys, densely packed with 50,000 people. Fifteen thousand of them are elderly Jews, including 10,000 Tsarist-era Eastern European refugees, the greatest such concentration in the world.

They mix today, uneasily, with 13,000 Latin American and 6,000 Muriel refugees.

South Beach is an area Miami Beach has forgotten. Property values are down. The crime rate is up. People live in abject poverty and total fear.

NEWSPAPER PHOTOGRAPHER OF THE YEAR, BILL FRAKES, THE MIAMI HERALD, ALL PHOTOS PPS. 168-171.

In the early evening (above) the older people gather together and rest on benches along the ocean. Woman at right is Francis Mitnick, who usually keeps her door chained. At far right, a hassidic Jew on the way to service.

*Carrying their chairs, a couple
heads for the beach to soak up the
sun.*

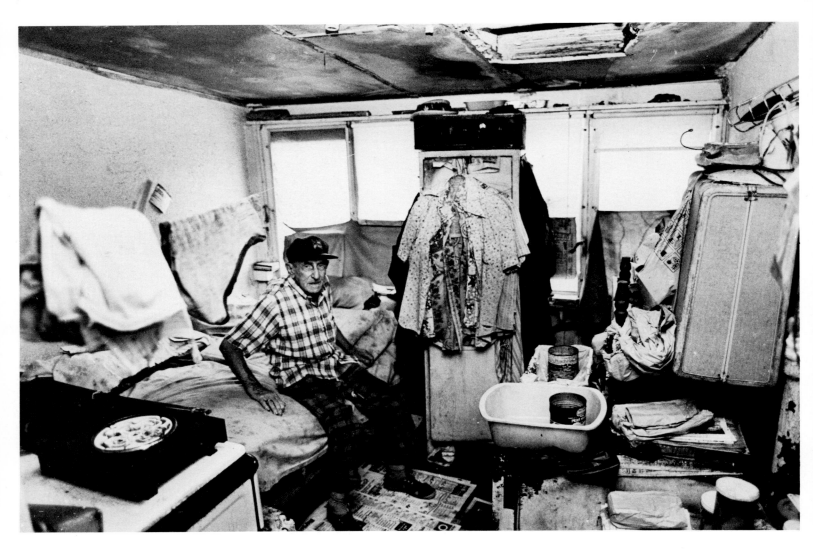

Benny Mazor (above) has lived in this $40-a-month room for 15 years. He has nowhere else to go. Compared to the concentration camps, he says, this room is a palace. Man in negligee (right) roams the streets. He won't wear pants; he's afraid the heat will cause cancer.

South Beach:

Benci Mendolsohn (above) with picture of his wife and son, made before they were arrested and taken to Auschwitz, where she was executed in a gas chamber. He never remarried. At left, an 80-year-old blind man and the dog he depends on share a quiet moment in a park.

LOUIE PSIHOYOS FOR TIME MAGAZINE

Say Cheese

In the marvelous clutter of events and circumstances that form the grist of the news photographer's mill, one subject dominates all the rest: People.

For, it is both trite and true that people really are most interested in other people. (Proof: the magazine of the same name.)

And so shooters spend a great deal of their working time seeking the telling photograph of the newsmaker, the compassionate picture of the person caught up in the whirlpool of violence, the revealing portraits of the Movers and Shakers as they let their guards down.

These next 30 pages contain some of the top selections from the Portrait/Personality category of the 1982 Pictures of the Year competition.

Dressed in the Victorian style first introduced by missionaries (left), an Herero woman sits on her front stoop. Dress shows both the merging nation of Namibia and its wildlife. (Original in color.)

Pope John Paul II lets his fatigue show in Madrid, after a week of heavy touring. (Original in color)

MAGAZINE PHOTOGRAPHER OF THE YEAR, JIM BRANDENBURG, NATIONAL GEOGRAPHIC

HONORABLE MENTION FEATURE PICTURE STORY, APRIL E. SAUL, THE PHILADELPHIA INQUIRER

SECOND PLACE MAGAZINE PORTFOLIO, HARRY BENSON, FREELANCE FOR LIFE

After doing "tons of stories" about women, Photographer April E. Saul thought she'd get rid of "old stereotypes about men," by shooting the life and times of a single father. Her subject, Jim Kollick, has four children. Story took nine months to shoot, including key photograph above.

After auto maker John DeLorean was jailed on charges of conspiring to import and distribute 220 pounds of cocaine, wife Christina was photographed at her home in New Jersey. She holds a picture taken of them in happier times.

FIRST PLACE PORTRAIT/PERSONALITY, MIKE SMITH, DALLAS TIMES HERALD

Photographer Mike Smith, assigned to do a story on the Texas Rangers, spent two days with Carl Weathers. Smith says Weathers is "the quintessential Texas Ranger, projecting the kind of image the Rangers prefer: confident, neatly dressed, well groomed."

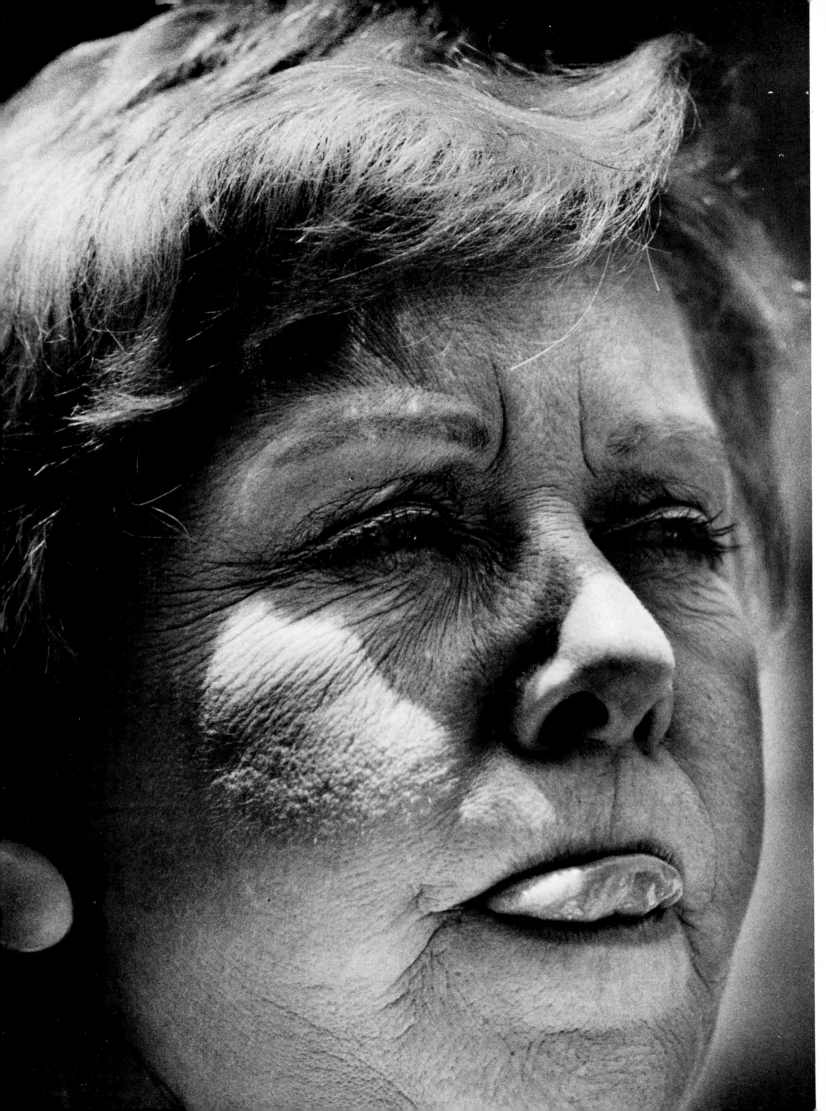

MICHAEL SCHWARTZ, FREELANCE, RIVERDALE, N.Y.

Chicago's Mayor Jane Byrne
attended a ground-breaking
ceremony, saw a friend, stuck her
tongue out, thought better of it.
But Photographer Thompson
caught some of the action.

GEORGE THOMPSON, CHICAGO TRIBUNE

New York's Mayor Ed Koch walked
the streets of his city as he sought
Democratic nomination for
governor. Photographer Schwartz
feels his photograph "epitomizes
the actor and crowd pleaser."

HONORABLE MENTION PORTRAIT/PERSONALITY, MARK SLUDER, THE CHARLOTTE, N.C., OBSERVER

*Marion Cannon: At 77 she's a poet, integrationist,
world citizen, life-long resident of Charlotte, N.C.
Photographer Mark Sluder's a native of Charlotte, too,
and volunteered to illustrate a profile of her. "That
setting is probably what Marion Cannon's soul is like,"
said Sluder, "a small tree sitting in the constant warmth
of light, producing fruit to nourish those she meets."*

HONORABLE MENTION SPOT NEWS, WILLIAM E. LYONS, THE NEW CASTLE, PA., NEWS

When Horace Bradley arrived at his new home in New
Castle, Pa., he was greeted with racist messages spray-
painted on the house, including a "KKK" on the door.
But when his new neighbors found out about the
vandalism, they volunteered to hold a painting party to
remove the obscenities. "I wanted to show that not
just a building was violated, but a human being also,"
Photographer William E. Lyons said.

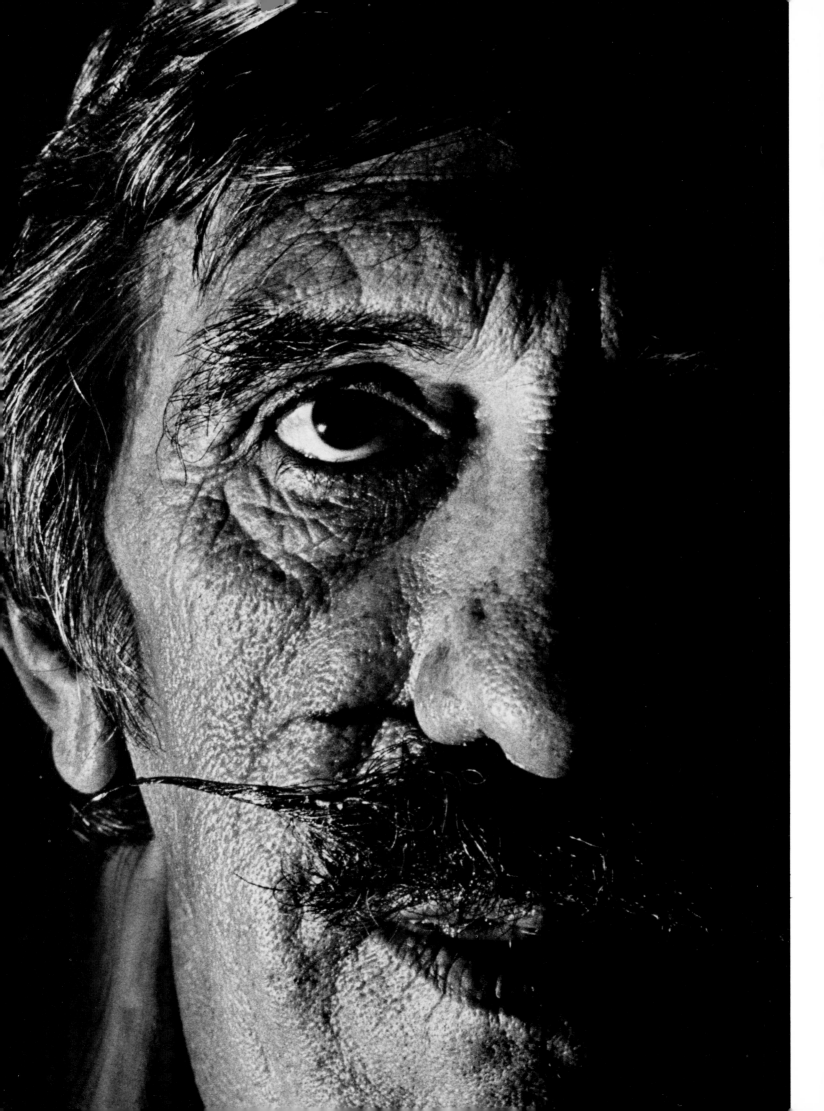

LINDA MC CONNELL, THE ROCKY MOUNTAIN NEWS

Bag lady, left, hadn't eaten for four days when Photographer Linda McConnell made this picture. McConnell spent the next two weeks with the woman, but the story ended abruptly when the woman decided the photographer was against her. Said McConnell: "The picture expresses her frustrations, but mine as well. She was someone who was sinking, that I could only watch go down."

THOM HALLS, THE FRESNO, CALIF., BEE

At 9, Penni Householder, right, knows how to deal with her handicap-ichthyosis, a rare and incurable skin disorder. It leaves her body scaly and she suffers from constant itching. Said Photographer Thom Halls: "I wanted to show the innocence of a little girl trapped."

Photographer Michael E. Keating made photograph, left, of a University of Cincinnati professor to go with a feature on homosexuality. It didn't run: "Too strong," said Keating.

MICHAEL E. KEATING, THE CINCINNATI ENQUIRER

JAY B. MATHER, COURIER-JOURNAL AND LOUISVILLE TIMES

Photographer Jay B. Mather believes the best time for closeups of drivers in the Indianapolis 500 is just before the race begins. "The trick is like betting on a horse race," Mather said. "Pick one and stay with your choice." Mather picked Gordon Johncock. It was a good choice: Johncock won.

In Olathe, Kan., this man wears a fire mask, too. He's a firefighter, Capt. Bill Dietzmen, who's better known by the nickname he wears on his helmet.

RANDY PENCH, SACRAMENTO, CALIF., BEE

The odds of twins living to be 100 are 700 million to one, according to the Guiness Book of World Records. Elizabeth Brown English and her twin sister, Lucy Brown Coleman (top left) beat the odds as they turned 100 in 1982.

Pete and Emilia Salazar (bottom left) both are nearly 100 years old. They have spent their lives in a tiny Colorado town. Photographer Anthony Suau wanted to show "the love and emotion that held them together for more than 75 years."

Photographer Randy Pench made this photograph of refugees to accompany a series on the hopes and hardships of Southeast Asians in a Sacramento suburb. This is 75-year-old Si Lu and her 2-year-old grandson, Din Voong. Said Pench: "Together, they symbolize the strong family ties that sustain the refugees."

Big cigar and electric hair are the trademarks of fight promoter Don King. Photographer Michael Mercanti got them both in this picture, taken at ringside during Atlantic City casino boxing match.

MARLIN LEVISON, MINNEAPOLIS STAR & TRIBUNE

Sig Olson, above, elder statesman of the Midwest's environmental movement, lights up in his log cabin on the Canadian border. "My favorite author," Photographer Marlin Levison called the 81-year-old nature writer. "Within a few months after I made this portrait, Sig Olson died in the snow on a trail ... strapping on his cross country snow skis," Levison said.

Ex-band leader and TV personality Desi Arnaz smokes a cigar as he floats in his pool, to talk about his return to film (Coppola's "Escape Artist"), after 25 years.

PATRICK DOWNS, LOS ANGELES TIMES-SAN DIEGO

Photograph of Kim Sue was made to accompany a story about the sale of an old Nevada brothel. Said Photographer Chris Hardy: "One of the most professional of the girls, Kim Sue says if you only bring in $20, you better bring it in hard."

THIRD PLACE PORTRAIT/PERSONALITY, CHRIS HARDY, SAN FRANCISCO EXAMINER

When Miami's last nude beach was closed in May 1982, it was Photographer William Snyder's first assignment to shoot a nude since his college days. The problem: How to present the subject subtly enough to get it past the editors. Not only did Snyder's photograph of this cheerful Yankee fan make his paper and the wire services — but the subject wanted extra copies.

WILLIAM SNYDER, THE MIAMI NEWS

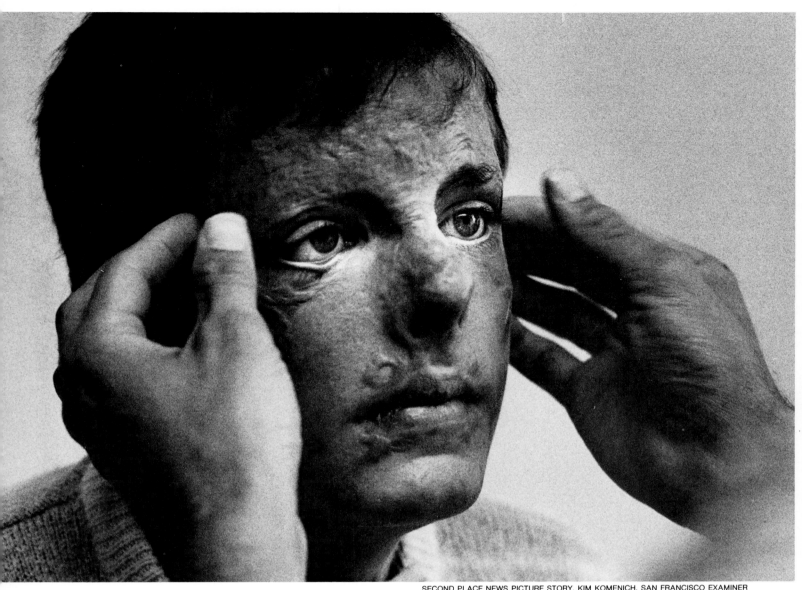

SECOND PLACE NEWS PICTURE STORY, KIM KOMENICH, SAN FRANCISCO EXAMINER

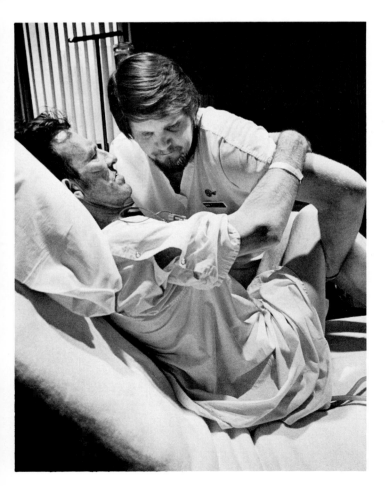

Long and painful job of reconstructive surgery began for 16-year-old Kelly Tyler, above, in the summer of 1982, three months after she sustained massive burns in an auto accident. Photographer Kim Komenich made pictures at the time Kelly was injured, then followed the story through the girl's treatment and her return to life as a normal schoolgirl.

Male nurses are not all that common in most American hospitals, but their ranks are growing. Nurse Bill Ritchie moves a patient, left. He's a nurse at the Methodist Hospital in Louisville, where, said Photographer Bill Luster, "He makes beds, walks patients and cares for their every need."

RUNNER-UP, NEWSPAPER PHOTOGRAPHER OF THE YEAR, BILL LUSTER, LOUISVILLE COURIER-JOURNAL AND TIMES

WILLIAM SERNE, ST. PETERSBURG, FLA., TIMES AND EVENING INDEPENDENT

RANDY OLSEN, SAN JOSE, CAL., MERCURY/NEWS

Valiant but unsuccessful- Rick Gardenshire competes in a hot dog contest at San Jose's Chili Cookoff, but lost when he stopped at eight.

MIMI FULLER FOSTER, CINCINNATI POST

On her way to shoot a tragic kidnapping follow-up, Photographer Mimi Fuller Foster stopped at a firemans' outing for its feature possibilities. Said Foster: "It was a relief to see THE picture right away, so I could leave."

That's a strum fiddle Dave Coombs of Tampa, Fla., is playing (left). Coombs was performing with a German band during an Oktoberfest celebration: "Hopping all over the stage with the beat," said Photographer William Serne.

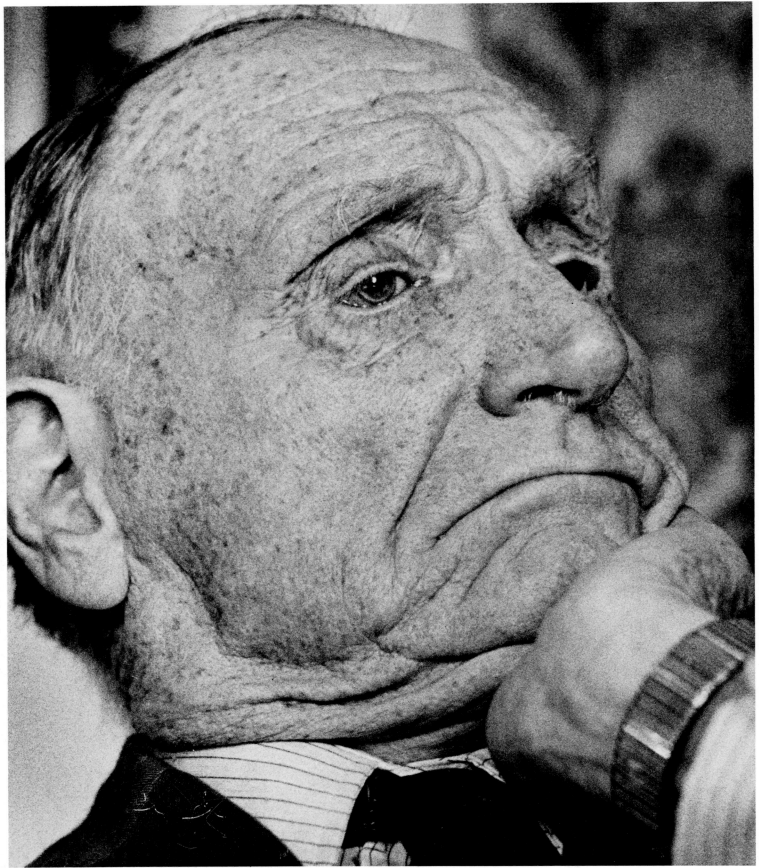

PAUL E. RODRIGUEZ, CLAREMONT, CALIF., COURIER

Same camera angle provides a study in contrasts. Robert Penn Warren, Pulitzer Prize-winning author and poet, ponders a question at a literary conference, while Comedian Red Skelton at 69 is busier than ever, making 125 appearances a year on campuses and in theaters all over the country.

TOM TONDEE, THE DAILY REPORT, ONTARIO, CALIF.

MAGAZINE SELF-EDITED PICTURE STORY, JIM BRANDENBURG, NATIONAL GEOGRAPHIC

JIM COLBURN, PHOTOREPORTERS, INC.

Portrait of Manchurian (above) is from National Geographic's massive, two-year project, "Journey Through China." It is an area, said Photographer Jim Brandenburg, "that has been shielded from the Western world for nearly 30 years." At right, a grim Gen. Voycek Jaruzelski considers Polish decision to lift martial law — which didn't particularly ease tensions in that country. Below, Artist Francesco Clemente.

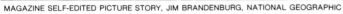

THIRD PLACE MAGAZINE PORTRAIT/PERSONALITY, GIANFRANCO GORGONI, GEO MAGAZINE

FIRST PLACE MAGAZINE PORTRAIT/PERSONALITY, HARRY BENSON, FREELANCE FOR LIFE

HONORABLE MENTION MAGAZINE PORTRAIT/PERSONALITY, JONATHAN BLAIR, NATIONAL GEOGRAPHIC

In a portrait from Photographer Harry Benson's feature on American Indians (above), 103-year-old Willie Frank Sr., sings to his 15-month-old granddaughter, Merita Miguel. At left, mud-covered Sicilian visitor to the island of Vulcano dries over hot steam vents in the earth.

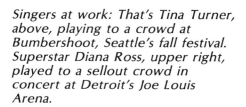

Singers at work: That's Tina Turner, above, playing to a crowd at Bumbershoot, Seattle's fall festival. Superstar Diana Ross, upper right, played to a sellout crowd in concert at Detroit's Joe Louis Arena.

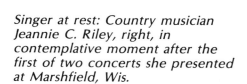

Singer at rest: Country musician Jeannie C. Riley, right, in contemplative moment after the first of two concerts she presented at Marshfield, Wis.

Amina Muhammad awoke in the West Bank settlement of Ferdis one night to see her wheat supply burning. The men moving away from the blaze wore Israeli uniforms. In the rubble she cries, "Is this justice? Why would they do this?"

RUNNERUP MAGAZINE PHOTOGRAPHER OF THE YEAR, HARRY BENSON, FREELANCE FOR PEOPLE MAGAZINE

RENEE C. BYER, THE PEORIA, ILL., JOURNAL STAR

Photographer Renee C. Byer had 10 minutes to make a picture of the winner of a seniors spelling bee in a nursing home. "I had a feeling of accomplishment for developing the assignment into more than was required," she said.

NEWSPAPER PHOTOGRAPHER OF THE YEAR BILL FRAKES, THE MIAMI HERALD

What can any caption writer add to this portrait of a 91-year-old Floridian with her pet?

197

Thousands of skiers from 30 countries participate in the 26-mile Engadine ski marathon in Switzerland every March. The winner will finish in about two hours.

FIRST PLACE MAGAZINE PICTORIAL WALTER IMBER, FOR GEO

Pope John Paul II paces in solitude atop the Apostolic Palace.

When fitness expert Jack LaLanne brought a free exercise clinic and fitness rally to Philadelphia, he demonstrated how to exercise the 55 muscles of the face. Every one of those muscles is 67 years old.

When diet-exercise pro Richard Simmons brought his philosophy and his demonstrations to the Rochester, N.Y., Institute of Technology, he not only told the folks how it should be done, he showed 'em.

KEVIN HIGLEY, GANNETT ROCHESTER [N.Y.] NEWSPAPERS

HONORABLE MENTION FASHION ILLUSTRATION, BO RADER, FLORIDA TIMES-UNION, JACKSONVILLE

Junk car, above, provides setting for Punk Fashion. At right, Photographer Pat McDonogh illustrated the versatility of sweat shirt material after designers began using it for everything from dresses to tank tops.

SECOND PLACE FASHION ILLUSTRATION, PAT MC DONOGH, FT. MYERS, FLA., NEWS-PRESS

THIRD PLACE FASHION ILLUSTRATION, BRUCE GILBERT, THE MIAMI HERALD

Photograph at left is an illustration for a story on the fashion rage of 1982: the tuxedo look. Photograph above illustrates fall fashion story with the theme, "Black Magic." Woman shown below is a Mongolian housewife photographed by James L. Stanfield while covering the Great Wall of China. "I wanted to photograph ... those people the Wall was built to keep out," Stanfield said.

FIRST PLACE FASHION ILLUSTRATION, PAT MC DONOGH, FT. MYERS, FLA., NEWS-PRESS

SECOND PLACE MAGAZINE PORTRAIT/PERSONALITY, JAMES L. STANFIELD, NATIONAL GEOGRAPHIC

Photograph of Gertrude Donahey was made to use with story marking her retirement as Ohio state treasurer. She was the first woman to hold a major elected office in Ohio and was, said Photographer Eric Albrecht, "very cooperative in posing," even though she hadn't expected a photographer at the interview.

SECOND PLACE, PORTRAIT/PERSONALITY, ERIC ALBRECHT, NEW PHILADELPHIA, OHIO, TIMES REPORTER

Photograph of Archbishop James Byrn of Dubuque, Iowa, was made to use with personality profile of one of the most powerful churchmen in the state. Photographer Bob Modersohn made two bounce flash frames of the cleric against his office door. Said Modersohn: "I guess I have an affinity to white walls."

HONORABLE MENTION PORTRAIT/PERSONALITY, BOB MODERSOHN, DES MOINES REGISTER

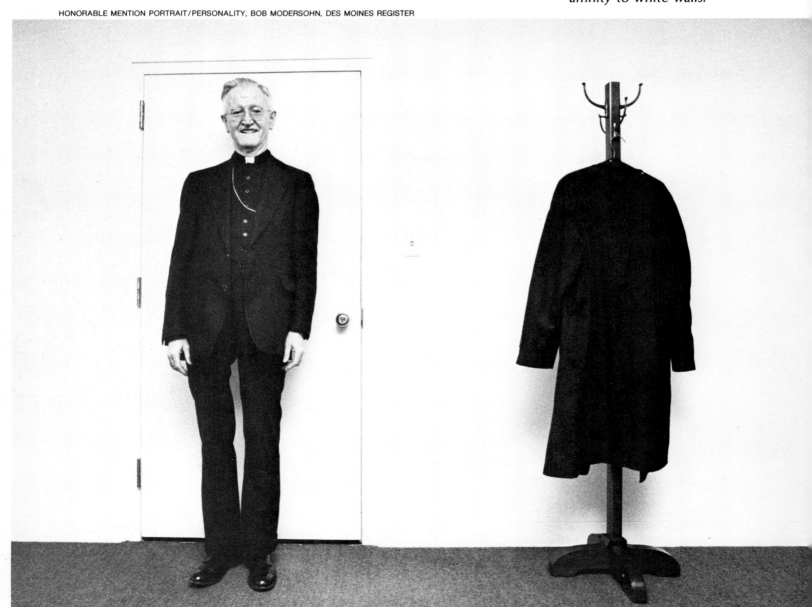

Contemplative pose, serene portraiture: Kathleen Turner, rising young actress, star of "Body Heat," and "The Man with No Brains."

Portrait of Lt. Gen. James A. Doolittle was made to commemorate the 40th anniversary of his famous air raid on Tokyo during World War II. Photographer Richard D. Green included just a suggestion of a globe in the foreground "because it occurred to me that this man just might have changed the world in a small way."

THIRD PLACE NEWSPAPER PHOTOGRAPHER OF THE YEAR CHRIS JOHNS, THE SEATTLE TIMES

Indian riders and their horses hit the chill Okanogan River, above, after a plunging ride down a 200-foot bank. It's the Suicide Race, part of a rodeo called the Omak Stampede in North Central Washington. Contrast that action with pre-game boredom of a minor league baseball game in Macon, Ga., right, where members of the Gastonia Cardinals wait for the umpire's call to play ball.

HONORABLE MENTION MAGAZINE SPORTS, DAVID BURNETT, GEO MAGAZINE

It's only a game

American fascination with sports showed no signs of lessening in 1982; on the contrary. Even with a 57-day strike of professional football players, there was sports action in plenty for fans, players . . . and photographers. Best of their efforts is shown on the next 44 pages.

FIRST PLACE MAGAZINE SPORTS, NATHAN BENN, NATIONAL GEOGRAPHIC

Contact sports have their less violent moments. At left, a boxer turns a suspended bag into a blur as he works out in a Miami Beach gym. Some of the gym's trainers are named on the old poster in the background. Below, Bryan Millard of Texas and Terry Crouch of Oklahoma head for their locker rooms at half time.

SECOND PLACE MAGAZINE SPORTS, JEFF JACOBSON, GEO MAGAZINE

ROBERT A. DEUTSCH, GANNETT WESTCHESTER NEWSPAPERS

Yankee great Craig Nettles just misses one of his patented stabs at a line drive during a game against the Minnesota Twins. "He used to make most of these," Photographer Bob Deutsch lamented, "but his age is starting to show."

Reach out . . .

At right, K.C. Chiefs wide receiver Henry Marshall makes a connection with Frank Wattelet, New Orleans Saints safety, on Marshall's touchdown run at the Superdome. Saints won, 27-17.

FRANK NIEMEIR, THE KANSAS CITY TIMES

Photographer Keith A. Myers made picture (above) of a floating Larry Drew, Kansas City Kings guard, on his first Kings assignment of the year. "I got lucky," said Myers.

THIRD PLACE SPORTS ACTION, DALE GULDAN, MILWAUKEE JOURNAL/SENTINEL

Tired of shooting second base action, Photographer Dale Guldan moved to a perch high above home plate to capture Brewer Paul Molitor evading Minnesota Twins Catcher Sal Butera's attempt to tag him out in a first-of-the-season game.

... *reach out* ...

It was one of those times when everyone was grabbing everyone else's face mask. But the Ram's Wendell Tyler (right) made the touchdown against Kansas City, and no penalty was called.

ROBERT LACHMAN, LOS ANGELES TIMES

JOHN LONG, HARTFORD COURANT

When Bloomfield, Conn., played Penney High of East Hartford for the state's Class M football title, Bloomfield's Darnell Ladson (above) ran away from a shirt-tail tackle to help his team win the game . . . and the championship.

RICHARD HEIN, DAILY SOUTHTOWN ECONOMIST, CHICAGO

Two New Orleans Saints defenders made a right angle out of Ken Margerum, a receiver for the Chicago Bears, in an NFL game played before the players' strike. It was not a happy time for either Margerum or the Bears; they lost this game and were one out of only 10 teams that didn't make the playoffs in the strike-shortened season.

When Scott Shipton's opponent in a high school championship wrestling match began using a bowling grip, Photographer Dale Duchesne said he spent the rest of the night "wondering how well I was focused." He was. Wrestler Shipton won, too.

DALE J. DUCHESNE, FINGER LAKES TIMES, GENEVA, N.Y.

. . . and touch someone.

Members of the Los Gatos girls basketball team went 16 feet (count 'em) off the floor when they won the Northern California championship game in a storybook finish, tying the game in the final 30 seconds, then going on to win. Photographer Eugene Louie made this exposure as the final buzzer sounded.

EUGENE LOUIE, SAN JOSE, CALIF., MERCURY-NEWS

The thrill . . .

Heavyweight boxer Michael Dokes literally walks on air as referee Davey Pearl stops his fight with Lynn Ball. The win gave Dokes the North American Boxing Federation heavyweight championship.

. . . of victory,

Darrel Porter, World Series Most Valuable Player, is sandwiched in celebration, right, after the St. Louis Cardinals beat Milwaukee in the seventh Series game. Porter's embracing Pitcher Bruce Sutter, who got two saves and a win in the Series.

FIRST PLACE SPORTS ACTION, RAYMOND GEHMAN, VIRGINIAN PILOT-LEDGER STAR, NORFOLK, VA.

An 800-meter race in Missoula, Mont. (above), went right to the ribbon. Photographer Raymond Gehman, then working for The Missoulian, said he "focused on the ribbon and waited for the moment."

Cross country runners were hosed down (right) at finish line during races at Notre Dame University. High temperatures and humidity caused so many runners to collapse that a fire truck was sent to help cool the athletes off.

. . . and the agony . . .

218

FIRST PLACE SPORTS FEATURE, DICK L. VAN HALSEMA JR., FLORIDA TIMES-UNION AND JACKSONVILLE JOURNAL

Studies in dejection: Morose youths above are members of the Sandalwood Saints baseball team in Jacksonville, after a one-point loss eliminated them from a tournament. Below, coach and players for the Nashville Sounds baseball team had nothing to say to each other during a June slump. Photographer Donnie Beauchamp said they "eventually snapped out of the slump and won the pennant or league or whatever."

HONORABLE MENTION SPORTS FEATURE, DONNIE BEAUCHAMP, THE NASHVILLE, TENN., BANNER

ERIC GAY, DENTON, TEX., RECORD-CHRONICLE

Depths of despair were touched by players of Pilot Point, Tex., High School, above. Not only did they lose a regional state playoff game, it was the team's first loss in three years.

A supine Richard Fortune of the Caroline Cavaliers, right, doesn't want to believe a last-second basket cost his team a semi-final game in Virginia's AA state basketball tournament.

. . . of defeat.

BILL KELLEY III, FREDERICKSBERG, VA., FREELANCE-STAR

DAYMON J. HARTLEY, FREELANCE FOR UPI

Going, going . . .

Detroit Lions' high-flying Billy Sims took to the air (left) over the New York Giants' defensive line, heading for the end zone in a mid-season game. He came to earth a yard short. Below, Mike Trapani, catcher for a suburban Chicago summer league team, came down back-first and minus the ball. Photographer Jon Langham said catcher's team was in the process of losing its 10th straight game.

JON A. LANGHAM, PIONEER PRESS, WILMETTE, ILL.

. . . gone.

On his first assignment to photograph a harness race (right) Photographer Dave Dieter first worked the crowd at a county fair in Fayettville, Tenn., swung his camera to the track when driver Ronnie Clyton's sulky wheel buckled. No injuries, said Dieter. Below, annual Memorial Day race in Moline, Ill., went fine until a light rain began to fall. Slick track wiped out biker Kurt Schabell.

DAVE DIETER, HUNTSVILLE, ALA., TIMES

THOMAS KIMMELL, THE DAILY DISPATCH, MOLINE, ILL.

It's goodby, ball, right, as Arizona's Rickey Walker and UCLA guard Kenny Fields hit the floor. UCLA recovered the ball and won the PAC-10 game.

Georgia's running back, Herschel Walker, is known for his high-flying approach to the goal line. "So instead of shooting him head on, I got down low to show how high he really gets," Photographer Bill Wax recalled. "And sure enough, he went up and over (right) for six points." The action came in the Florida-Georgia game in Jacksonville, Fla., in which Walker made three touchdowns. Georgia won, 44-0.

Six University of Washington defense men, left, were in on this tackle of Oregon quarterback Mike Jorgensen in a late September PAC-10 game in Seattle. The Huskies lost.

MARICE CAROLYN COHN, THE MIAMI HERALD

Football players at Miami's Killian High School work on their reflexes. "Just like a chorus line practicing to get their moves straight," said Photographer Marice Cohn.

With an hour between assignments, Photographer Donald S. Fisher found 7 and 8-year-olds playing league baseball for the first time, below, and having trouble with their attention span.

DONALD S. FISHER, THE EXPRESS, EASTON, PA.

AL. S. PODGORSKI, THE DAILY PANTAGRAPH, BLOOMINGTON, ILL.

Referee Frank Strocchia frantically signals time out after official Rich McVay went down during University of Illinois-Michigan State game at Champaign, Ill. A Big 10 official since 1974, McVay was pronounced dead at the hospital. "Rich had always said he wanted to die while refereeing a game on national TV," Photographer Al Podgorski said. "I did not feel good taking shots of the course of events."

California Angels Pitcher Tommy John collided with Umpire Bill Kunkel as he ran to first base to cover a throw. Kunkel, seated, called the runner out. "John agreed," said Photographer Brad Graverson. (The Angels won, too, defeating the Milwaukee Brewers 8-3 in the first game of the American League championship series.)

BRAD A. GRAVERSON, THE DAILY BREEZE, TORRANCE, CALIF.

RUNNER-UP, NEWSPAPER PHOTOGRAPHER OF THE YEAR, BILL LUSTER, COURIER-JOURNAL AND LOUISVILLE TIMES

Girl Jock

The only person who objected when Beth Bates went out for the high school football team at Williamsburg, Ky., was her brother, a quarterback. "He thought," said Photographer Bill Luster, "she might beat him out of a position."

But Beth made the team- as a kicker-the first female to play football in Kentucky on a varsity level.

Luster spent two days on Beth's story, found she was "a player who enjoyed the company of her teammates, and also enjoyed being a girl."

At left, Beth lifts weights to strengthen her legs.

Beth has to dress out of her car (lower left). She puts on her trousers at home, dons the rest of the uniform at the playing field. She's allowed in the locker room just before the game, then waits on sidelines until it's time for her specialty.

She kicks, dances

Beth "high fives" a teammate on the sidelines after her team whipped rival Berea High School 66-14. She kicked two extra points in the game. After the game, right, Beth and her boyfriend enjoy the homecoming dance.

Kids throwing leather ... little boys

Amateur boxers at the Sheridan Club in Des Moines, Iowa, come in several sizes, including the smallest of them all: Kids as young as five, who tip the scale at a mere 40 pounds.

These pint-sized gladiators wear pillow-sized gloves and padded headgear. Their bouts go three 30-second rounds. Mothers and fathers watch as the baby tigers flail away, urging them on with screams of "Crack him again, Mikey. Kill him. Knock him down."

Neither parents nor trainer think there's any damage suffered by the tiny boxers, either mental or physical. Says the club manager: "Boxing is good for them. It teaches them self-defense and keeps them off the streets."

But Dr. Marilee Fredericks, director of the Des Moines Child Guidance Center, feels otherwise: "The idea of little kids pounding on each other with parents shrieking and urging them on makes me feel uneasy. It's at this age that we're trying to put the brakes on aggression and violent impulses."

Photographer Dave Peterson said his story "tried to raise some serious questions about the legitimacy of boxing as a sport for 5, 6, and 7-year-old children. I may have become more sensitive than usual because I have a 5-year-old son."

Some of the boys have to stand on a chair to reach the speed bag.

mix it up in the ring

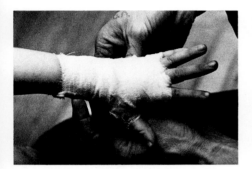 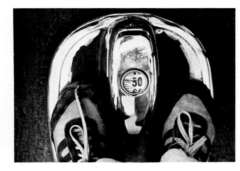

FIRST PLACE SPORTS PICTURE STORY, DAVE PETERSON, DES MOINES REGISTER (ALL PHOTOS PPS. 232-235)

Mike Henderson, 6, is comforted during a workout by Tommy Thompson, who heads the Sheridan Club. Mike was sparring and got punched in the nose. Thompson says injuries are rare among the younger kids.

Tiny boxers—

Parents and friends scream wildly during matches that, said Peterson, "resemble cock fights." At right, 6-year-old sits in his corner and waits for the bell.

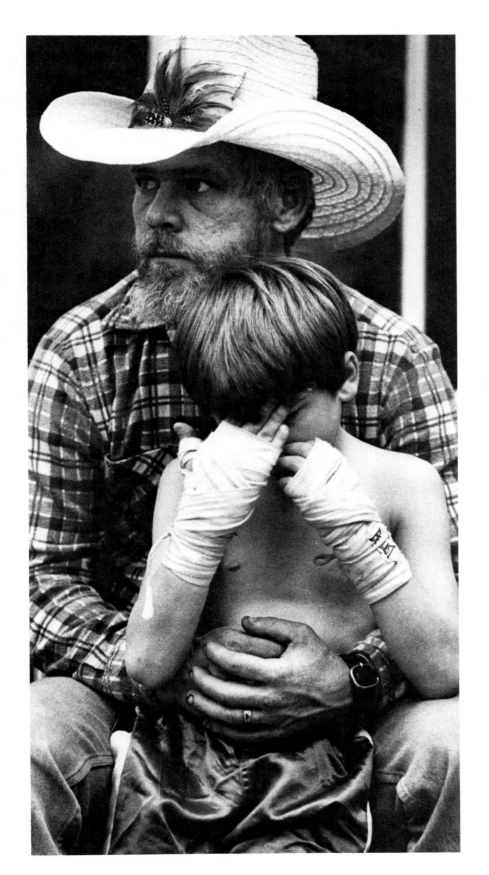

A father comforts his son after his three-round match.

LARRY REESE, HOUSTON CHRONICLE

Kids who caught calves in a scramble at the Houston Livestock Show and Rodeo got to keep them. It was the first time girls could try, but Kim Williams (above) just couldn't control the critter; on the contrary.

Whoa, dammit!

Contestants in a wild horse race at the Ellensburg, Wash., Rodeo tried hard to control their steed, but couldn't. Not only that, the horse "just missed kicking me in the head," said Photographer Larry Steagall.

LARRY STEAGALL, YAKIMA (WASH.) HERALD REPUBLIC

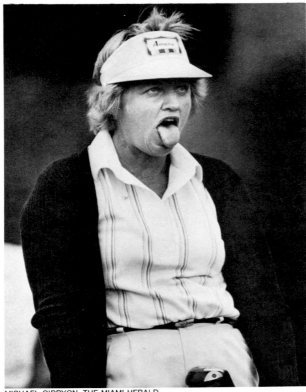

Sometimes a subject doesn't say a word, but the message still comes through, loud and clear. At left, golf pro Joanne "Big Mamma" Carner watches her drive during final match of Whirlpool Championship in Deerfield Beach, Fla. (She lost.) Below, light-heavyweight champ Dwight Braxton lets challenger Matthew Saad Muhammad know what the (still) champion thinks about Muhammad's pre-fight predictions. At right, high school hurdler Lance Reed of Willingboro, N.J., High School competes in a state hurdles event. (He didn't win.)

MICHAEL O'BRYON, THE MIAMI HERALD

DICK BELL, PHILADELPHIA INQUIRER

DENNIS MC DONALD, BURLINGTON COUNTY, N.J., TIMES (RIGHT)

RUTGERS UNIVERSITY

BUDDY NORRIS, DAILY PRESS, NEWPORT NEWS, VA.

Slammin' Sammy Snead blasts out of a sand bunker during pro-am at Williamsburg, Va. A lucky combination, said Photographer Buddy Norris, that "just happened" to include the grandaddy of all pro golfers.

Hammin' Sammy Davis Jr., reacts to a muffed putt during Greater Hartford pro-am. Photographer Paula Bronstein followed Davis for six holes and said this shot "made it worth while."

PAULA BRONSTEIN, NEW HAVEN REGISTER/JOURNAL COURIER

Milwaukee pitcher Don Sutton allowed seven runs in five innings of the sixth World Series game in St. Louis. Manager Harvey Kuenn went out to pull Sutton, left, just as it began to rain. Sutton thumbed himself out. Below left, Missouri basketball coach Norm Stewart gets positive with a couple of his players during game against defending national champs North Carolina. It must have worked: The Missouri Tigers won. Below, Don Zimmer, manager of the Texas Rangers, can only watch as his team loses yet another game. Said Photographer Edward J. Hille: "The team was so bad that even the paying customers were going to sleep. Zimmer was fired the next day."

EDWARD J. HILLE, THE DALLAS MORNING NEWS

FRANK NIEMEIR, THE KANSAS CITY TIMES

JIM WAKEHAM, COLUMBIA MISSOURIAN

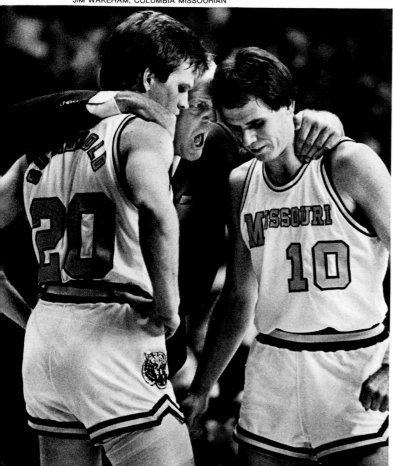

SECOND PLACE SPORTS ACTION, DAVE WILLIAMS, WICHITA EAGLE-BEACON.

THIRD PLACE SPORTS FEATURE, RICH ADDICKS, ATLANTA NEWSPAPERS

Underwater hockey in a YWCA swimming pool — one of the lesser-known sports covered in zoned editions of Photographer Dave Williams' paper, the Wichita Eagle-Beacon. At left, a classic situation: 13-year-old Steve Stanton waits in the Atlanta Falcon's locker room, hoping to catch an autograph from Falcon Matthew Teague after the interview's over.

'We're number one!'

Milwaukee fans went wild when the Brewers won the American League pennant Oct. 10. Photographer Dale Guldan covered the championship game (against the California Angels), then wandered downtown to Wisconsin Avenue, "where I found people literally hanging from the lampposts, deliriously happy."

ERIC LUSE, SAN FRANCISCO CHRONICLE

San Francisco officials figured 35,000 persons would greet the 49rs if they won the Super Bowl. Wrong — half a million persons jammed downtown streets to celebrate. Three floors above the wild scene, Photographer Eric Luse got this telling picture, avoided what he called "a very dangerous situation."

'So are we!'

RUNNER-UP NEWSPAPER PHOTOGRAPHER OF THE YEAR, BILL LUSTER, COURIER-JOURNAL AND LOUISVILLE TIMES

When former Kentucky Gov. A.B. "Happy" Chandler was inducted into the Baseball Hall of Fame at Cooperstown, N.Y., Photographer Bill Luster was on hand to record the event; after all, Luster's photographed Chandler, baseball's second commissioner, almost yearly since 1969. "A fascinating man," said Luster.

DAVE DIETER, HUNTSVILLE, ALA., TIMES

That long shadow was cast by a
sports legend: Paul "Bear" Bryant,
the University of Alabama's football
coach, who compiled a 323-85-17
record in 38 years. Photographer
Dave Dieter made this picture of
Bryant several weeks before the
Bear's retirement in November
1982. The shadow as prophetic; he
died Jan. 26, 1983.

Judging the 40th

MICHAEL O'BRIEN left the Miami News in 1979 to freelance out of New York City. Runner-up Photographer of the Year in 1979, he holds numerous photo awards.

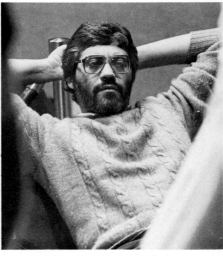

ROBERT PLEDGE: English born, French raised, he reported on Third World affairs, headed photo agency Gamma, founded Contact Press Images in 1976.

Early in 1983 the five persons shown here spent four days in a room at the University of Missouri's School of Journalism. There, they judged some 20,000 photographs entered in the 40th annual Pictures of the Year competition. Winners of that judging, plus selected additional pictures, comprise the content of this volume.

The 40th POY was a record-setter: More photographers entered (almost 1,600); more photographs, more time spent in judging.

A common judging complaint: Conventionality, similarity of entries. At the same time, winners were praised for their immediacy and believability.

One judge's assessment

By Barbara London

About the middle of the first day judging photographs for the 1982 Pictures of the Year competition, several things occurred to me. First of all, the magnitude of the job struck me. Here it was only a few hours into the judging and I had already made Yes/No decisions on several thousand pictures. How was I ever to find the psychic stamina to bring a fair judgment to the 20,000 more pictures, which I would see in the next few days? After regaining some energy (lunch is always a rejuvenator), I then began to notice that many pictures fell into categories. For example:

-The Don't Jump Photo: Camera angling up at the ledge of a building where one person is reaching an arm out toward another person.

-The Disaster Photo: Person in the foreground clutching another person or a pet or some possession while the house is burning or floating away in the background.

-The Something's in the Wrong Place Photo: Like the woman with her hand stuck in the toilet or the car embedded in the side of the house.

-The Burning Building Photo: Printed very dark so that the firefighters are silhouetted against the flames. Another popular fire scene is the fireman in winter with water frozen onto his hat.

-The Retarded Person Doing Something Photo. This category requires some explanation. In the worst of its type, the retarded person is on display, performing for the photographer and by extension for the viewer: Look, I can run a race, or Look, I know how to dress myself. The pictures in this category are too often afflicted with a benevolent voyeurism that seems well intentioned, but off the mark. They do at least serve a useful purpose in exposing the general public to the needs and achievements of a retarded people, but even better would be a heartfelt understanding that passes beyond categorizing the retarded as "them" and the photographer and viewer as "us"

I am not ridiculing any of these situations. What I am pointing out is what we often do not notice: that many photographs show us the world in standardized ways or patterns. We have forgotten how we learned from these patterns or even that we learned them at all. Anthropologists tell about certain tribes seeing photographs for the first time. When handed a photograph of another member of their own tribe, these people not only cannot identify the subject, but cannot even see the photograph as a representation of a human being. They have to be taught to decipher the photographic conventions that we take for granted.

SUSAN KISMARIC is associate curator, Department of Photography, Museum of Modern Art, New York, has lectured in Japan on photo trends.

BOB LYNN: Director of photography, Virginian-Pilot & Ledger-Star, Norfolk, Va. He's the winner of numerous national photography and writing awards.

BARBARA LONDON: Author, publisher of books on photography that have sold in excess of 1 million copies. She's a partner in the firm of Curtin & London.

In the POY judging, these conventional forms were unavoidably brought to my attention. I saw so many pictures within such a short period of time that it was impossible to ignore how similar some of them were. After I had seen seven or eight examples of the I'm All Grown Up Now Photo (young child dressed in mommy's clothes or clutching a big hammer or the like), the ninth or tenth example raised very little interest. I had seen too many like it already.

That is the problem with conventional forms. Although they are convenient and easily comprehended, their overuse dulls our awareness and eventually bores us. Photographers are not the only ones who use them to excess. The French poet Mallarme wrote: "The common use of language is like the exchange of a coin whose obverse and reverse no longer bear any but worn effigies, and which people pass from hand to hand in silence." So it went with many of the pictures.

Then it would happen. Yet another I'm All Grown Up Now Photo, but this one .. this one is different. Maybe it is the expression: the photographer caught that moment when the child had a particularly sly look, as if she was going to take the hammer and *break* something.

Or, along comes one more sequence of photos on the daily life of a retarded person. But this one touches me in a way that

other, similar photographs have not. The person seems real. The photographer genuinely contacted the individual and so conveys that contact to me. I can feel the struggle to get to the finish line of the Special Olympics race or can appreciate the effort this person put into combing his hair. I no longer stand outside the person's life looking at it, but move into the pictures and become part of that life.

Sometimes a graphic element caught my eye. A boxer is working out on a punching bag, and the photograph strikingly contrasts the blur of his motion against sharply focused lettering on the gym wall behind him (see page 207).

One photograph stood out because it is a classic of its kind-The Airplane Disaster Photo (see page 10). A black cloud of smoke billows from the big jet crashed in the background. The plane lies in the stubble of a field, looking as out of place and helpless as a beached whale. The survivors, some grieving, others in shock, move along a path curving to the foreground. The picture combines the intensity of the moment with strong graphic composition, and is so perfectly visualized that I could imagine it as a still from a disaster movie, set up to evoke emotion plus have pictorial appeal.

The pictures that attracted my attention, the pictures that stand out in my memory, and many of the pictures that were selected as

winners, are those that reveal the particulars, the uniqueness of a scene. They achieve an intimacy with the subject. They go beyond the typical view of a situation to show it to me as if the photographer was experiencing it for the first time.

What makes one photograph better than another is what the photographer brings to the scene-a willingness to risk contact with the subject, an ability to notice something unusual, an ingenuity in finding a new way to show a standard event. All these are skills that can be learned, but can't be taught. They grow as the photographer grows.

Simply looking at photographs stretches one's vision. Before the POY judging, I had seen many, many photographs, but never this many variations on a photojournalist's themes: conflict, victory, defeat, love, pain and so on. After POY, if I ever take up the photojournalist's trade, I ought to at least know when I am taking a picture that has been done over and over in a similar fashion. And after POY, I now admire even more those photographs- and those photographers- that show me something in a way that I have not seen before.

I didn't have to worry, after all, about finding the psychic stamina to finish the judging. It came from the periodic pleasure of seeing the best photographs themselves.

The Winners:

Newspaper division:

SPOT NEWS:
First - Murry Sill, Miami Herald, "Swift Justice"
Second - Mary Schroeder, Detroit Free Press, "Terror at the Buhl Building"
Third - Darlene Pfister, Minneapolis Star & Tribune, "Their friend was murdered"
Honorable mention - William E. Lyons, New Castle News, Pa., "Moving day"
Honorable mention - Karen T. Borchers, San Jose, Calif., Mercury/News, "Handcuffs and a kiss"
Honorable mention - Timothy R. Aubry, Associated Press, "Got away"

GENERAL NEWS:
First - Karen Elshout, St. Louis Post Dispatch, "Out of work"
Second - Jebb Harris, Courier-Journal and Louisville Times, "Anguish and honor: Vietnam veterans memorial dedication"
Third - Robert Fila, Chicago Tribune, "A last look"
Honorable mention - Anne Cusack, Chicago Tribune, "After the fire"
Honorable mention - Eli Reed, San Francisco Examiner, "Dead rebels - Guatemala"
Honorable mention - Jose M. More, Chicago Tribune, "Why me?"

FEATURE PICTURE:
First - William K. Dab, Providence Journal-Bulletin, "Bear ballet"
Second - Michael J. Bryant, San Jose Mercury News, "Hanging too loose"
Third - Charlaine Brown, Orange County Register, Santa Ana, Calif., "Watching 'em take it off"

Honorable mention - Eric Luse, San Francisco Chronicle, "All fired up"

SPORTS ACTION:
First - Raymond Gehman, Virginian-Pilot/Ledger Star, Norfolk, Va., "Race to the ribbon"
Second - Dave Williams, Wichita Eagle-Beacon, "Underwater scramble"
Third - Dale Guldan, Milwaukee Journal, "Safe!"
Honorable mention - Scott Henry, Las Vegas Review Journal, "Jump for joy"

SPORTS FEATURE:
First - Dick L. Van Halsema Jr., Florida Times-Union & Jacksonville Journal, "The fallen Saints"
Second - Edward J. Ballotts Jr., South Bend, Ind., Tribune, "The agony"
Third - Rich Addicks, Atlanta Constitution-Journal, "Impatient autographer"
Honorable mention - Donnie Beauchamp, Nashville Banner, "Dejected baseball players"

PORTRAIT PERSONALITY:
First - Mike Smith, Dallas Times Herald, "Tying one on"
Second - Eric Albrecht, New Philadelphia, Ohio, Times-Reporter, "Retiring state treasurer"
Third - Chris Hardy, San Francisco Examiner, "My old flame"
Honorable mention - Robert J. Modersohn III, Des Moines Register, "The archbishop is ready to see you now"
Honorable mention - Mark B. Sluder, Charlotte, N.C. Observer, "Marion Cannon"

PICTORIAL:
First - Scott Goldsmith, Courier-Journal and Louisville Ky., Times, "Leader of the band"
Second - David Pickel, Daily Press/Times-Herald, Newport News, Va., "Sunset on the Vietnam era"
Third - Pat Crowe, Wilmington, Del., News-Journal, "Romp in the fog"
Honorable mention - Dick L. Van Halsema Jr., Florida Times-Union and Jacksonville Journal, "Intermission cleanup"

FOOD ILLUSTRATION:
First - Pat McDonogh, Ft. Myers, Fla., News-Press, "Cold pasta salad"
Second - George Wedding, San Jose Mercury/News, "Blessed are the bagels"
Third - Craig Hartley, Houston Post, "Light wine"

FASHION ILLUSTRATION:
First - Pat McDonogh, Ft. Myers News-Press, "The tuxedo look"
Second - Pat McDonogh, Ft. Myers News-Press, "The sweat shirt style"
Third - Bruce Gilbert, Miami Herald, "Black magic, fall fashion"
Honorable mention - Bo Rader, Florida Times-Union and Jacksonville Journal, "Punk to junk"

EDITORIAL ILLUSTRATION:
No first, second or third places awarded.
Honorable mention - Chuck Isaacs, Philadelphia Inquirer, "Vanishing unwed fathers"
Honorable mention - Bern Ketchum, Topeka Capital-Journal, "Women in this man's army"

NEWS PICTURE STORY:
First - Jebb Harris, Courier-Journal and Louisville Times, "Anguish and honor: Vietnam veterans memorial"

Second - Kim Komenich, San Francisco Examiner, "To hell and back"
Third - James L. Davis, Arizona Daily Star, Tucson, "Shootings in Miracle Valley"

FEATURE PICTURE STORY:
First - Karen Kasmauski, Virginian-Pilot/Ledger-Star, Norfolk, Va., "Myra, just a lady, please"
Second - Neil McGahee, Minneapolis Star & Tribune, "Charley and Wilhelm"
Third - Michael S. Wirtz, Dallas Times Herald, "The Ervay shine and domino parlor"
Honorable mention - Judy Griesedieck, Hartford Courant, "The hotel Hartford"
Honorable mention - April Saul, Philadephia Inquirer, "Jim Kolick, single father"

SPORTS PICTURE STORY:
First - David Peterson, Des Moines Register, "Scars unseen"
Second - Bill Luster, Louisville Courier Journal & Times, "Louisville Redbirds' mascot"
Third - Bill Luster, Louisville Courier Journal & Times, "Joining baseball's immortals"

SELF-PRODUCED PUBLISHED PICTURE STORY — BROADSHEET:
First - Nancy Warnecke, The Tennessean, Nashville, "Brides of Christ"
Second - Bill Wax, Gainesville Sun, "63 years together"
Third - Richard Marshall, Ithaca, N.Y., Journal, "The range riders"

SELF-PRODUCED PUBLISHED PICTURE STORY — TABLOID:
First - Joe Patronite, Arizona Daily Star, Tucson, "Tiny miracles"
Second - John Metzger, Ithaca Journal, "Road to glory"
Third - A. J. Sundstrom, freelance, "The trappists"

Magazine division:

NEWS OR DOCUMENTARY:
First - Werner Voight, Sipa Press/Black Star for LIFE, "Plane crash in Malaga"
Second - Yan Morvan, Sipa Press/Black Star for LIFE, "PLO departure from Beirut"
Third - Gino Zamboni, freelance for LIFE, "Riot in Brussels"
Honorable mention - Stephen R. Brown, U.S. News & World Report, "Phosphorous burn victim"
Honorable mention - Anonymous, Gamma-Liaison for Newsweek, "Death of a general"

FEATURE:
First - H. Peter Curran, freelance for New York Times Magazine, "Jesuit confession in Micronesia"
Second - Thomas Haley, Visions for GEO, "Butlers"
Third - Diana H. Walker, Time, "Honorees"

SPORTS:
First - Nathan Benn, National Georgraphic, "Boxing shadows"
Second - Jeff Jacobson, freelance for GEO, "Football: Texas-Oklahoma"

Third - Tobey Sanford, freelance for LIFE, "Body builders"
Honorable mention - David Burnett, Contact Press Images for GEO, "Gastonia Cardinals"
Honorable mention - Franco Zehnder, freelance for GEO, "Ski race"

PORTRAIT/PERSONALITY:
First - Harry Benson, freelance for LIFE, "Indians"
Second - James L. Stanfield, National Georgraphic, "Nangsilama, Mongolian housewife"
Third - Gianfranco Gorgoni, Contact Press Images for GEO, "Francesco Clemente"
Honorable mention - Norman Seeff, freelance for GEO, "Francis Crick"
Honorable mention - Jonathan Blair, National Georgraphic, "Volcanic man"

PICTORIAL:
First - Walter Imber, freelance for GEO, "The Vatican"
Second - Phil Schofield, freelance for National Georgraphic, "Winter farm scene"
Third - Thomas Nebbia, National Georgraphic "Journey into China"

Magazine Winners (cont'd)

Honorable mention - Jodi Cobb, National Geographic, "Footloose in China"

SCIENCE/NATURAL HISTORY:
First - Jim Brandenburg, National Georgraphic, "Gemsbok in dunes"
Second - Chuck O'Rear, National Georgraphic, "Computer in the hand"
Third - Joseph Daniel, freelance for New York Times Magazine, "Africa - slash burning"

PUBLISHED PICTURE STORY:
First - John Loengard, LIFE, "Shooting past 80"

Second - Kazoyoshi Nomachi, Photo Researchers for LIFE, "People of the Southern Sudan"
Third - Barbara Bordnick, freelance for GEO, "Lines from the chorus"
Honorable mention - Phil Schofield, freelance for National Geographic, "Paradise called the Palouse"

SELF-EDITED PICTURE STORY:
First - Louie Psihoyos, National Geographic, "Urban ore"
Second - Jim Brandenburg, National Geographic, "Manchuria"
Third - Robin Moyer, Black Star for TIME, "Lebanon, June-November, 1982"

Editing Awards:

BEST USE OF PHOTOGRAPHS BY A NEWSPAPER:
The Seattle Times

NEWSPAPER PICTURE EDITOR AWARD:
David M. Yarnold, San Jose Mercury News

NEWSPAPER-MAGAZINE PICTURE EDITOR AWARD:
David M. Yarnold, Cal Today (San Jose Mercury News)

BEST USE OF PHOTOGRAPHS BY A MAGAZINE:
National Geographic
Judges' special recognition: Camera Arts

MAGAZINE PICTURE EDITOR AWARD:
Bruce A. McElfresh, National Georgraphic

BEST USE OF PHOTOGRAPHS BY A NEWSPAPER: SEATTLE TIMES

BEST USE OF PHOTOGRAPHS BY A MAGAZINE: THE NATIONAL GEOGRAPHIC

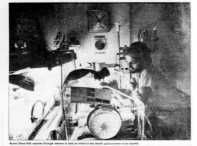

TINY MIRACLES

THE UNIT

NEWSPAPER SELF-PRODUCED PICTURE STORY (TABLOID):
JOE PATRONITE, ARIZONA DAILY STAR, TUCSON, "TINY MIRACLES"

EISENSTAEDT

MAGAZINE PUBLISHED PICTURE STORY,
JOHN LOENGARD, LIFE, "SHOOTING PAST 80"

State/Metro A Thanksgiving Story
The Sisters of St. Cecilia

The Brides of Christ

A Striving To Be One With God

Text and photos by NANCY WARNECKE

'Wherever God Leads, Be Thankful'

NEWSPAPER SELF-PRODUCED PICTURE STORY
(BROADSHEET): NANCY WARNECKE, THE TENNESSEAN
(NASHVILLE), "BRIDES OF CHRIST"

THE PASSAGE TO PRIESTHOOD

STORY BY EDWARD O. WELLES • PHOTOGRAPHY BY MICHAEL J. BRYANT

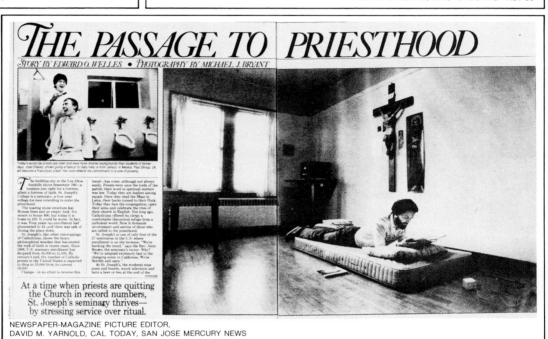

At a time when priests are quitting
the Church in record numbers,
St. Joseph's seminary thrives—
by stressing service over ritual.

NEWSPAPER-MAGAZINE PICTURE EDITOR,
DAVID M. YARNOLD, CAL TODAY, SAN JOSE MERCURY NEWS

SATURDAY SPECTRUM

Call 'em Coasties

The recruits graduate as a team...minus 11

NEWSPAPER PICTURE EDITOR (LEFT),
DAVID M. YARNOLD, SAN JOSE MERCURY NEWS

Camera Arts

GREAT PHOTOGRAPHERS AT WORK
André Kertész: Roots of a Modern Master
Bruce Davidson's Subway Photos/Hamaya's Mountains
Brett Weston's Artistry in the Darkroom

Camera Arts

Workshop in Studio Lighting Techniques
Classic Portraits from the Great Days of *Vanity Fair*
Color Landscape Photographs from the Air

Camera Arts

Learn from a Master: Walker Evans at Work
Fashion Fantasies by Rebecca Blake · Photo Books
Cover Story: Pierre Cordier's Chemigrams

SPECIAL RECOGNITION, BEST USE OF PHOTOGRAPHS BY A MAGAZINE, CAMERA ARTS

MAGAZINE PICTURE EDITOR (RIGHT),
BRUCE A. MC ELFRESH, NATIONAL GEOGRAPHIC

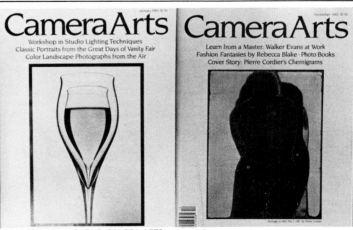

Preserving a Mountain Heritage

By SIR EDMUND HILLARY

Index to photographers

BILL SANDERS, FORT LAUDERDALE, FLA., NEWS AND SUN SENTINEL

But what have you got for tomorrow?